## IN PRAISE OF ROY PETER CLARK'S
# Writing Tools

"For all the aspiring writers out there — whether you're writing a novel or a technical report — a respected scholar pulls back the curtain on the art. 'Think of writing as carpentry,' he says, 'and consider this book your toolbox.'"
— Teresa K. Weaver, *Atlanta Journal-Constitution*

"I wish I'd had *Writing Tools* when I began my life as a writer — not only because it would have spared me so much anguish, but because it would have helped me have a hell of a lot more fun."
— Adrian Nicole LeBlanc, author of *Random Family*

"Superlative. . . . The advice is practical, sharp, and hefty. What makes it a pleasure to read is that the prose proves and demonstrates the principles as it goes, morphing a list-shaped book into a page-turner with some out-loud laughs."
— Janet Burroway, *St. Petersburg Times*

"For a long time, Roy Peter Clark has had more faith than anyone I know (including me) in the premise that people can be taught to write well. Now he has gone and written a book that shows exactly how. *Writing Tools* offers advice and lessons that will help me, my students, and anyone with the dream of becoming a better writer."
— Mark Bowden, author of *Black Hawk Down* and *Guests of the Ayatollah*

"Would that I had had Clark's manual when I wrote my first book, *Dead Man Walking*. This book, replete with incisive techniques and strategies, also includes a mentor: Clark's guiding voice is on every page. Writers couldn't ask for a better teacher."
— Sister Helen Prejean, author of *Dead Man Walking*

"In *The Elements of Style,* Professor William Strunk gaveled English usage to order and E. B. White elevated its style. Now the ebullient Roy Peter Clark sets the lyrics of the language to playful music and lets it dance. His *Writing Tools* fits on the same shelf as Strunk and White and lends it some streetwise fun. . . . Americans from college student to memo-mangling CEO need this one on the desk. It's not just a helpful handbook to sort out awkward writing. It's a public service."
— Eugene C. Patterson, Pulitzer Prize–winning editor and retired chairman and CEO, *St. Petersburg Times*

"What a relief to read a handbook about writing that stresses tools, not rules, that shows what you *can* do as a writer as opposed to what you should do. . . . The book is beautifully carpentered, the prose equivalent of a Shaker table, which I predict will hold up to continued and hard use as the years go by and it mellows into both a classic and a keeper."
— Madeleine Blais, Pulitzer Prize–winning journalist and author of *In These Girls, Hope Is a Muscle* and *Uphill Walkers*

"In this terrific book, Roy Peter Clark helps us see that what we secretly hoped is true — that any person, at any stage, can become a better writer. . . . Every writer should have this book on her desk. It's destined to become a classic."
— Diana K. Sugg, Pulitzer Prize–winning reporter, *Baltimore Sun*

"This is the most useful book of its kind I've seen since William Zinsser's *On Writing Well.* The format is lucid and concise. The examples are brilliantly chosen. And Roy Peter Clark's brief explanatory essays are models of the writer's craft. A masterwork from a master teacher."
— David Von Drehle, author of *Triangle: The Fire That Changed America*

"Pull out a favorite novel or short story, and read it with the guidance of Clark's ideas. . . . Readers will find new worlds in familiar places. And writers will be inspired to pick up their pens."
— *Boston Globe*

"What a nifty book! It's not only useful, central, wise, rigorous, and forgiving, it's also a riot. The author's quirky Buddha-nature shines through."
— Mark Kramer, director of the Nieman Program on Narrative Journalism, Harvard University

"Clark is a joyful, brilliant teacher who unlocks the mysteries of literary flow. This book is one to keep near the keyboard."
— Anne Hull, national reporter for the *Washington Post*

"There are 'born writers' in this world, sometimes as many as two or three a century. The rest of us have to work at it. That means thinking analytically about the skills we need to acquire. Roy Clark has been doing just that for over thirty years and generously sharing his insights in the classroom, in the newsroom, and in his popular workshops. Now he has given writers of every kind fifty 'tools' to improve our work. Here's a fifty-first: buy this book!"
— Howell Raines, journalist and author of *The One That Got Away*

"Roy is the Obi-Wan Kenobi of writing teachers. . . . Like its author, *Writing Tools* is brilliant, openhearted, and indispensable; it's easily one of the best books ever published about our craft."
— Thomas French, Pulitzer Prize–winning journalist and author of *Unanswered Cries* and *South of Heaven*

"This is a useful tool for writers at all levels of experience, and it's entertainingly written, with plenty of helpful examples."
— David Pitt, *Booklist*

# Writing Tools

## 50 Essential Strategies for Every Writer

## Roy Peter Clark

LITTLE, BROWN AND COMPANY

NEW YORK   BOSTON   LONDON

Little, Brown and Company

Hachette Book Group

237 Park Avenue, New York, NY 10017

www.littlebrown.com

Originally published in hardcover by Little, Brown and Company, September 2006
First paperback edition, January 2008

Little, Brown and Company is a division of Hachette Book Group, Inc.
The Little, Brown name and logo are trademarks of Hachette Book Group, Inc.

The publisher is not responsible for websites (or their content) that are not owned by the publisher.

"Uncle Jim" from Liquid Paper: New and Selected Poems, by Peter Meinke, © 1991. Reprinted by permission of the University of Pittsburgh Press.

Library of Congress Cataloging-in-Publication Data

Clark, Roy Peter.
Writing tools : 50 essential strategies for every writer / Roy Peter Clark. — 1st ed.
   p. cm.
Includes index.
ISBN 978-0-316-01498-4 (hc) / 978-0-316-01499-1 (pb)
1. Authorship.   2. English language — Rhetoric.   I. Title.
PN145.C63  2006
808'.042 — dc22                                        2006014607

20 19 18 17 16 15 14 13
RRD-C

Design by Meryl Sussman Levavi

Printed in the United States of America

*To Donald M. Murray*

*and to the memory of Minnie Mae Murray,*

*godparents to a nation of writers*

# Contents

―◁○▷―

## Part Two. SPECIAL EFFECTS 57

## Part Three. BLUEPRINTS 117

## Part Four. USEFUL HABITS 193

# Writing Tools

# A Nation of Writers

Americans do not write for many reasons. One big reason is the writer's struggle. Too many writers talk and act as if writing were slow torture, a form of procreation without arousal and romance — all dilation and contraction, grunting and pushing. As New York sports writer Red Smith once observed, "Writing is easy. All you do is sit down at a typewriter and open a vein." The agony in Madison Square Garden.

If you want to write, here's a secret: the writer's struggle is overrated, a con game, a cognitive distortion, a self-fulfilling prophecy, the best excuse for not writing. "Why should I get writer's block?" asked the mischievous Roger Simon. "My father never got truck driver's block."

Good readers may struggle with a difficult text, but struggle is not the goal of reading. The goal is fluency. Meaning flows to the good reader. In the same way, writing should flow from the good writer, at least as an ideal.

The ability to read, society tells us, contributes to success in education, employment, and citizenship. Reading is a democratic craft. Writing, in contrast, is considered a fine art. Our culture taps only a privileged few on the shoulder. *We* are the talented ones, and you're not. The teacher read *our* stories aloud in class, or encouraged *us* to enter an essay contest, or pushed *us* toward the newspaper or literary magazine. We thrive on such recognition, but think of the millions left behind.

If you feel left behind, this book invites you to imagine the act of writing less as a special talent and more as a purposeful craft. Think of writing as carpentry, and consider this book your toolbox. You can borrow a writing tool at any time, and here's another secret: Unlike hammers, chisels, and rakes, writing tools never have to be returned. They can be cleaned, sharpened, and passed along.

These practical tools will help to dispel your writing inhibitions, making the craft central to the way you see the world. As you add tools to your workbench, you'll begin to see the world as a storehouse of writing ideas. As you gain proficiency with each tool, and then fluency, the act of writing will make you a better student, a better worker, a better friend, a better citizen, a better parent, a better teacher, a better person.

I first gathered these tools at the Poynter Institute, a school for journalists, but thanks to the Internet they have traveled around the world and back. They have found their way into the hands of teachers, students, poets, fiction writers, magazine editors, students, freelancers, screenwriters, lawyers, doctors, technical writers, bloggers, and many other workers and professionals who traffic in words. To my surprise, online versions are being translated into several languages, including Italian, Spanish, Portuguese, Russian, Arabic, Japanese, and Indonesian, reminding me that writing strategies can and do cross boundaries of language and culture.

You will find in this toolbox new ways of thinking, along with many familiar pieces of advice, dusted off and reframed for a new century. But where do writing tools come from?

• *From great works on writing, such as* The Elements of Style *and* On Writing Well. These tools took a lifetime to gather, and not just mine. They took the lifetimes of Dorothea Brande, Brenda Ueland, Rudolf Flesch, George Orwell, William Strunk and his student E. B. White, William Zinsser, John Gardner, David Lodge, Natalie Goldberg, Anne Lamott, and all generous authors who share their knowledge about how good writing is made.

• *From the authors whose works, more than two hundred of them, are sampled here.* Using a method of close reading, I find a passage that intrigues me, put on my X-ray glasses, and peer beneath the surface of the text to view the invisible machinery of language, syntax, rhetoric, and critical thinking that creates the effects I experience as a reader. I then forge what I see into a writing tool.

• *From productive conversations with professional writers and editors.* I once learned that only three behaviors set literate people apart. The first two are obvious: reading and writing; but the third surprised me: talking about how reading and writing work. Many of the tools came from great talk about the construction of stories and the distillation of meaning.

• *Finally, from America's great writing teachers.* They have labored for decades to demystify the writing process for students, to describe writing as a craft, a set of rational steps, a box full of tools, habits, and strategies.

I reveal these sources — great works about writing, the effective work of writers, good talk among writers and editors, tools passed on by teachers — not only to give due credit, but also to offer the means and methods by which to gather a lifetime of writing tools. As Chaucer wrote more than six hundred years ago: "The life so short, the craft so long to learn."

Before I open *Writing Tools* for your inspection, let me suggest ways to use this book:

- *Remember, these are tools, not rules.* They work outside the territory of right and wrong, and inside the land of cause and effect. Don't be surprised when you find many examples of good writing in the world that seem to violate the general advice described here.

- *Do not try to apply these tools all at once.* Aspiring golfers swing and miss if they try to remember the thirty or so different elements of an effective golf swing. I promise you a case of writing paralysis if you think about too many of these tools when you sit down to write. Let your writing flow early. You can reach for a tool later.

- *You will become handy with these tools over time.* You will begin to recognize their use in the stories you read. You will see chances to apply them when you revise your own work. With time, they will become part of your process, natural and automatic.

- *You already use many of these tools without knowing it.* You cannot think, speak, write, or read without them. But now these tools will have names, so you can talk about them in different ways. As your critical vocabulary grows, your writing will improve.

You will notice that I have drawn examples of good writing from several genres of writing and storytelling: from fiction and poetry, from journalism and nonfiction, from essays and memoirs. The range is important. The literature reveals the best work that could be created under any circumstances, the journalism the best created under the exacting limits of time, space, and civic purpose. The testimony of many readers persuades me that tools in this book apply to the general tasks of most writers.

*Writing Tools* presumes some familiarity with the principles of standard English usage, grammar, punctuation, and syntax, but I have held technical language to a minimum. To gain full benefit, you should be able to identify the parts of speech, subjects and verbs, and the main clause of a sentence, and know the difference between active and passive voice. If you lack that knowledge, please read this book anyway. It will still help you improve your writing and will make clear what else you need to learn.

When a good friend first read these tools, he noted that they carried the writer and reader on a journey from the subatomic to the metaphysical level, from where to put the subject and verb to how to find your mission and purpose. That comment inspired a division of the tools into four boxes:

1. *Nuts and bolts:* strategies for making meaning at the word, sentence, and paragraph levels
2. *Special effects:* tools of economy, clarity, originality, and persuasion
3. *Blueprints:* ways of organizing and building stories and reports
4. *Useful habits:* routines for living a life of productive writing

At the end of each tool, you will find a set of workshop questions and exercises, more than two hundred in all. I wrote these with the student and teacher in mind, but I encourage everyone to read them, even if you do not perform the suggested task. They will help you imagine ways to grow as a writer.

Now that you know the contents and structure of this book, I'd like to enlist you to stand behind its mission and purpose. You will notice that my title, *Writing Tools,* is modest, but the title of this introduction, "A Nation of Writers," is bold. It's hard enough to imagine a village or colony of writers, but a nation? Why not?

Look around you. The National Commission on Writing has described the disastrous consequences of bad writing in America — for businesses, professions, educators, consumers, and citizens. Poorly written reports, memos, announcements, and messages cost us time and money. They are blood clots in the body politic. The flow of information is blocked. Crucial problems go unsolved. Opportunities for reform and efficiency are buried.

The Commission calls for a "revolution" in the way Americans think about writing. The time is right. Students now face high-stakes writing tests to advance in school and enter college. But technology stands on our side, easing the burdens of drafting and revision. I wrote my first book in 1985 on a Royal Standard typewriter. A machine just like it sits in my office, a museum piece. Now young writers use cell phones to communicate in the telegraphic and acronymic language of instant messages; words flash around the world with breathtaking speed. These new writers have created millions of Web logs and Web sites, becoming publishers of their own work.

No doubt, the standards expressed in these new forms are looser than those suggested by Strunk and White. The voices are more casual, the approaches more experimental, and the personae of the authors more elusive. These new voices cross old boundaries and command attention, but who would argue that the quality of writing online is what it could be? As these new writers mature, they will need writing tools to perfect their work.

We need lots of writing tools to build a nation of writers. Here are fifty of them, one for every week of the year. You get two weeks for vacation.

Learn and enjoy.

—◆◦◆—

# PART ONE

# Nuts and Bolts

◄o►

# Begin sentences with subjects and verbs.

*Make meaning early, then let weaker*
*elements branch to the right.*

Imagine each sentence you write printed on the world's widest piece of paper. In English, a sentence stretches from left to right. Now imagine this. A writer composes a sentence with subject and verb at the beginning, followed by other subordinate elements, creating what scholars call a *right-branching sentence.*

I just created one. Subject and verb of the main clause join on the left ("a writer composes") while all other elements branch to the right. Here's another right-branching sentence, written by Lydia Polgreen as the lead of a news story in the *New York Times:*

> Rebels seized control of Cap Haitien, Haiti's second largest city, on Sunday, meeting little resistance as hundreds of residents cheered, burned the police station, plundered food from port warehouses and looted the airport, which was quickly closed. Police officers and armed supporters of President Jean-Bertrand Aristide fled.

That first sentence contains thirty-seven words and ripples with action. The sentence is so full, in fact, that it threatens to fly apart like an overheated engine. But the writer guides the reader by capturing meaning in the first three words: "Rebels seized control." Think of that main clause as the locomotive that pulls all the cars that follow.

Master writers can craft page after page of sentences written in this structure. Consider this passage by John Steinbeck from *Cannery Row,* describing the routine of a marine scientist named Doc (the emphasis is mine):

> *He didn't need* a clock. *He had been working* in a tidal pattern so long that he could feel a tide change in his sleep. In the dawn *he awakened,* looked out through the windshield and saw that the water was already retreating down the bouldery flat. *He drank* some hot coffee, ate three sandwiches, and had a quart of beer.

> *The tide goes out* imperceptibly. *The boulders show* and seem to rise up and the ocean recedes leaving little pools, leaving wet weed and moss and sponge, iridescence and brown and blue and China red. On the bottoms *lie the incredible refuse* of the sea, shells broken and chipped and bits of skeleton, claws, the whole sea bottom a fantastic cemetery on which the living scamper and scramble.

Steinbeck places subject and verb at or near the beginning of each sentence. Clarity and narrative energy flow through the passage, as one sentence builds on another. He avoids monotony by including the occasional brief introductory phrase ("In the dawn") and by varying the lengths of his sentences, a writing tool we will consider later.

Subject and verb are often separated in prose, usually because we want to tell the reader something about the subject before we get to the verb. This delay, even for good reasons, risks confusing the reader. With care, it can work:

> *The stories* about my childhood, the ones that stuck, that got told and retold at dinner tables, to dates as I sat by red-faced, to my own children by my father later on, *are* stories of running away.

So begins Anna Quindlen's memoir *How Reading Changed My Life*, a lead sentence with thirty-one words between subject and verb. When the topic is more technical, the typical effect of separation is confusion, exemplified by this clumsy effort:

> *A bill* that would exclude tax income from the assessed value of new homes from the state education funding formula *could mean* a loss of revenue for Chesapeake County schools.

Eighteen words separate the subject, "bill," from its weak verb, "could mean," a fatal flaw that turns what could be an important civic story into gibberish.

If the writer wants to create suspense, or build tension, or make the reader wait and wonder, or join a journey of discovery, or hold on for dear life, he can save subject and verb of the main clause until later. As I just did.

Kelley Benham, a former student of mine, reached for this tool when called on to write the obituary of Terry Schiavo, the woman whose long illness and controversial death became the center of an international debate about the end of life:

> Before the prayer warriors massed outside her window, before gavels pounded in six courts, before the Vatican issued a statement, before the president signed a midnight law and the Supreme Court turned its head, *Terri Schiavo was* just an ordinary girl, with two overweight cats, an unglamorous job and a typical American life.

By delaying the main subject and verb, the writer tightens the tension between a celebrated cause and an ordinary girl.

This variation works only when most sentences branch to the right, a pattern that creates meaning, momentum, and literary power. "The brilliant *room collapses*," writes Carol Shields in *The Stone Diaries,* leaving a solid block of darkness. Only her *body survives,* and the problem of what to do with it. *It has not turned* to dust. A bright, droll, clarifying *knowledge comes over* her at the thought of her limbs and organs transformed to biblical dust or even funereal ashes. Laughable.

And admirable.

## WORKSHOP

1. Read through the *New York Times* or your local newspaper with a pencil in hand. Mark the locations of subjects and verbs.

2. Do the same with examples of your writing.

3. Do the same with a draft you are working on now.

4. The next time you struggle with a sentence, rewrite it by placing subject and verb at the beginning.

5. For dramatic variation, write a sentence with subject and verb near the end.

# Tool 2

—◄o►—

# Order words for emphasis.

*Place strong words at the beginning and at the end.*

Strunk and White's *The Elements of Style* advises the writer to "place emphatic words in a sentence at the end," an example of its own rule. The most emphatic word appears at "the end." Application of this tool will improve your prose in a flash.

For any sentence, the period acts as a stop sign. That slight pause in reading magnifies the final word, an effect intensified at the end of a paragraph, where final words often adjoin white space. In a column of type, a reader's eyes are likewise drawn to the words next to the white space. Those words shout, "Look at me!"

Emphatic word order helps the writer solve the thorniest problems. Consider this opening for a story in the *Philadelphia Inquirer.* The writer, Larry King, must make sense of three powerful elements: the death of a United States senator, the collision of aircraft, and a tragedy at an elementary school:

> A private plane carrying U.S. Sen. John Heinz collided with a helicopter in clear skies over Lower Merion Township yesterday, triggering a fiery, midair explosion that rained burning debris over an elementary school playground.

Seven people died: Heinz, four pilots and two first-grade girls at play outside the school. At least five people on the ground were injured, three of them children, one of whom was in critical condition with burns.

Flaming and smoking wreckage tumbled to the earth around Merion Elementary School on Bowman Avenue at 12:19 p.m., but the gray stone building and its occupants were spared. Frightened children ran from the playground as teachers herded others outside. Within minutes, anxious parents began streaming to the school in jogging suits, business clothes, house-coats. Most were rewarded with emotional reunions, amid the smell of acrid smoke.

On most days, any of the three elements would lead the paper. Combined, they form an overpowering news tapestry, one that reporter and editor must handle with care. What matters most in this story? The death of a senator? A spectacular crash? The deaths of children?

In the first paragraph, the writer chooses to mention the senator and the crash up front, and saves "elementary school playground" for the end. Throughout the passage, subjects and verbs come early — like the locomotive and coal car of an old railroad train — saving other interesting words for the end — like a caboose.

Consider also the order in which the writer lists the anxious parents, who arrive at the school in "jogging suits, business clothes, house-coats." Any other order weakens the sentence. Placing "house-coats" at the end builds the urgency of the situation: parents racing from their homes dressed as they are.

Putting strong stuff at the beginning and end helps writers hide weaker stuff in the middle. In the passage above, notice how the writer hides the less important news elements — the who and the when ("Lower Merion Township yesterday") — in the middle of the lead. This strategy also works for attributing quotations:

"It was one horrible thing to watch," said Helen Amadio, who was walking near her Hampden Avenue home when the crash occurred. "It exploded like a bomb. Black smoke just poured."

Begin with a good quote. Hide the attribution in the middle. End with a good quote.

Some teachers refer to this as the *2-3-1 tool of emphasis*, where the most emphatic words or images go at the end, the next most emphatic at the beginning, and the least emphatic in the middle, but that's too much calculus for my brain. Here's my simplified version: put your best stuff near the beginning and at the end; hide weaker stuff in the middle.

Amy Fusselman provides an example with the first sentence of her novel, *The Pharmacist's Mate:* "Don't have *sex on a boat* unless you want to *get pregnant.*" The most intriguing words come near the beginning and at the end. Gabriel García Márquez uses this strategy at the opening of *One Hundred Years of Solitude* to dazzling effect: "Many years later, *as he faced the firing squad,* Colonel Aureliano Buendía was to remember that distant afternoon when his father took him to *discover ice.*"

What applies to the sentence also applies to the paragraph, as Alice Sebold demonstrates in this passage: "*In the tunnel where I was raped,* a tunnel that was once an underground entry to an amphitheater, a place where actors burst forth from underneath the seats of a crowd, a girl had been murdered and dismembered. I was told this story by the police. In comparison, they said, I was *lucky.*" That final word resonates with such pain and power that Sebold turns it into the title of her memoir, *Lucky.*

These tools of emphasis are as old as rhetoric itself. Near the end of Shakespeare's famous tragedy, a character announces to Macbeth: "The Queen, my lord, is dead." This astonishing example of the power of emphatic word order is followed by one of the darkest passages in all of literature. Macbeth says:

> She should have died hereafter;
> There would have been a time for such a word.

Tomorrow, and tomorrow, and tomorrow
Creeps in this petty pace from day to day,
To the last syllable of recorded time;
And all our yesterdays have lighted fools
The way to dusty death. Out, out, brief candle!
Life's but a walking shadow, a poor player
That struts and frets his hour upon the stage
And then is heard no more. It is a tale
Told by an idiot, full of sound and fury,
Signifying nothing.

The poet has one great advantage over those who write prose. He knows where the line will end. He gets to emphasize a word at the end of a line, a sentence, a paragraph. We prose writers make do with the sentence and the paragraph — signifying something.

## WORKSHOP

1. Read Lincoln's Gettysburg Address and Dr. Martin Luther King Jr.'s "I Have a Dream" speech and study emphatic word order.

2. With a pencil in hand, read an essay you admire. Circle the first and last words in each paragraph.

3. Do the same for recent examples of your work. Revise sentences so that powerful and interesting words, which may be hiding in the middle, appear near the beginning and at the end.

4. Survey your friends to get the names of their dogs. Write these in alphabetical order. Imagine that this list appears in a story. Play with the order of the names. Which should go first? Which last? Why?

# TOOL 3

‹o›

## Activate your verbs.

*Strong verbs create action,*
*save words, and reveal the players.*

President John F. Kennedy testified that a favorite book was *From Russia with Love,* the 1957 James Bond adventure by Ian Fleming. This choice revealed more about JFK than we knew at the time and created a cult of 007 that persists to this day

The power of Fleming's prose flows from active verbs. In sentence after sentence, page after page, England's favorite secret agent, or his beautiful companion, or his villainous adversary, performs the action of the verb (the emphasis is mine):

> Bond *climbed* the few stairs and *unlocked* his door and *locked* and *bolted* it behind him. Moonlight *filtered* through the curtains. He *walked* across and *turned* on the pink-shaded lights on the dressing-table. He *stripped* off his clothes and *went* into the bathroom and *stood* for a few minutes under the shower. . . . He *cleaned* his teeth and *gargled* with a sharp mouthwash to get rid of the taste of the day and *turned* off the bathroom light and *went* back into the bedroom. . . .
>
> Bond *gave* a shuddering yawn. He *let* the curtains drop back into place. He *bent* to switch off the lights on the dressing-table. Suddenly he *stiffened* and his heart *missed* a beat.

There had been a nervous giggle from the shadows at the back of the room. A girl's voice *said,* "Poor Mister Bond. You must be tired. Come to bed."

In writing this passage, Fleming followed the advice of his countryman George Orwell, who wrote of verbs: "Never use the passive where you can use the active."

I learned the distinction between active and passive voice as early as fifth grade. Thank you, Sister Katherine William. I failed to learn, until much later, why that distinction mattered. But let me first correct a popular misconception. The voice of verbs (active or passive) has nothing to do with the tense of verbs. Writers sometimes ask, "Is it ever OK to write in the passive tense?" *Tense* defines action within time — *when* the verb happens — the present, past, or future. *Voice* defines the relationship between subject and verb — who does what.

- If the subject performs the action of the verb, we call the verb *active.*
- If the subject receives the action of the verb, we call the verb *passive.*
- A verb that is neither active nor passive is a *linking verb,* a form of the verb *to be.*

All verbs, in any tense, fit into one of those three baskets.

News writers reach often for the simple active verb. Consider this *New York Times* lead by Carlotta Gall on the suicidal desperation of Afghan women:

Waiflike, draped in a pale blue veil, Madina, 20, *sits* on her hospital bed, bandages covering the terrible, raw burns on her neck and chest. Her hands *tremble.* She *picks* nervously at the soles of her feet and confesses that three months earlier she *set* herself on fire with kerosene.

Both Fleming and Gall use active verbs to power their narratives, but notice an important difference between them. While Fleming uses the past tense to narrate his adventure, Gall prefers the present. This strategy immerses readers in the immediacy of experience, as if we were sitting — right now — beside the poor woman in her grief.

Both Fleming and Gall avoid verb qualifiers that attach themselves to standard prose like barnacles to the hull of a ship:

| | |
|---|---|
| sort of | seemed to |
| tend to | could have |
| kind of | used to |
| must have | begin to |

Scrape away these crustaceans during revision, and the ship of your prose will glide toward meaning with speed and grace.

The earnest writer can overuse a writing tool. If you shoot up your verbs with steroids, you risk creating an effect that poet Donald Hall derides as "false color," the stuff of adventure magazines and romance novels. Temperance controls the impulse to overwrite.

In *The Joy Luck Club*, novelist Amy Tan exercises exquisite control, using strong verbs to depict the authentic color of emotional truth:

> And in my memory I can still *feel* the hope that *beat* in me that night. I *clung* to this hope, day after day, night after night, year after year. I would *watch* my mother lying in her bed, babbling to herself as she *sat* on the sofa. And yet I *knew* that this, the worst possible thing, would one day *stop*. I still *saw* bad things in my mind, but now I *found* ways to change them. I still *heard* Mrs. Sorci and Teresa having terrible fights, but I *saw* something else. . . . I *saw* a girl complaining that the pain of not being seen was unbearable.

Ian Fleming's verbs describe external action and adventure; Amy Tan's verbs capture internal action and emotion. But action can also be intellectual, in the force and power of an argument, as Albert Camus demonstrates in *The Rebel:*

> The metaphysical rebel *protests* against the condition in which he *finds* himself as a man. The rebel slave *affirms* that there is something in him that will not *tolerate* the manner in which his master *treats* him; the metaphysical rebel *declares* that he is frustrated by the universe.

Notice that even with all the active verbs in that passage, Camus does not pass on the passive when he needs it ("he is frustrated"), which brings us to the next tool.

## WORKSHOP

1. Verbs fall into three categories: active, passive, and forms of the verb *to be*. Review your writing and circle verb forms with a pencil. In the margins, categorize each verb.

2. Convert passive and *to be* verbs into the active. For example, "It was her observation that" can become "She observed."

3. In your own work and in the newspaper, search for verb qualifiers and see what happens when you cut them.

4. Experiment with both voice and tense. Find a passage you have written in the active voice and in the past tense. Change the verbs to the present tense and consider the effect. Does it seem more immediate?

5. I described three uses of the active voice: to create outward action, to express inner or emotional action, and to energize an argument. Look for examples of all three in your reading and for opportunities to use them in your writing.

—◄o►—

# Be passive-aggressive.

*Use passive verbs to showcase*
*the "victim" of action.*

So the gold standard for writing advice is this: use active verbs. Those three words have been uttered in countless writing workshops with such conviction that they must be gospel. But are they?

Check out that last paragraph. In the first clause, I use a form of the verb *to be*, in this case "is." In the next sentence, I use the passive voice: "have been uttered." In the final sentence, I resort to another form of *to be*, in this case "are." My point is that you can create acceptable prose, from time to time, without active verbs.

Why, then, does voice matter? It matters because of the different effects active, passive, and *to be* verbs have on the reader and listener. I'll call on John Steinbeck again to describe this true-life encounter in North Dakota (the emphasis is mine):

> Presently I *saw* a man leaning on a two-strand barbed-wire fence, the wires fixed not to posts but to crooked tree limbs stuck in the ground. The man *wore* a dark hat, and jeans and long jacket washed palest blue with lighter places at knees and elbows. His pale eyes *were frosted* with sun glare and his lips scaly as snakeskin. A .22 rifle *leaned* against the fence beside him and on the ground *lay* a little heap of fur and feathers — rabbits and small

birds. I *pulled* up to speak to him, *saw* his eyes *wash over* Rocinante, *sweep up* the details, and then *retire* into their sockets. And I *found* I *had* nothing to say to him . . . so we simply *brooded* at each other. (from *Travels with Charley*)

I count thirteen verbs in that passage, twelve active and one passive, a ratio George Orwell would admire. The litany of active verbs heats up the scene, even though not much happens. The active verbs reveal who is doing what. The author sees a man. The man wears a hat. The author pulls up to talk with him. They brood at each other. Even inanimate objects perform action. The rifle leans against the fence. Dead animals lie on the ground.

Embedded in all that verbal activity is one splendid passive verb: "His pale eyes *were frosted* with sun glare." Form follows function. The eyes, in real life, received the action of the sun, so the subject receives the action of the verb.

That's the writing tool: use passive verbs to call attention to the receiver of the action. When columnist Jeff Elder described the extinction of an American species, the passenger pigeon, in the *Charlotte Observer,* he used passive verbs to paint the birds as victims: "Enormous roosts *were gassed* from trees. . . . They *were shipped* to market in rail car after rail car. . . . In one human generation, America's most populous native bird *was wiped out.*" The birds do nothing. They are done unto.

The best writers make the best choices between active and passive. A few paragraphs from the one cited above, Steinbeck wrote, "The night was loaded with omens." Steinbeck could have written, "Omens loaded the night," but in that case the active voice would have been unfair to both the night and the omens, the meaning and the music of the sentence.

In *Pedagogy of the Oppressed,* Brazilian educator Paulo Freire uses the distinction between active and passive verbs to challenge an educational system that places the power of teachers over the needs of students. An oppressive educational system, he argues, is one in which:

- the teacher teaches and the students are taught;
- the teacher thinks and the students are thought about;
- the teacher disciplines and the students are disciplined.

In other words, an oppressive system is one in which the teacher is active and the students are passive.

A strong active verb can add dimension to the cloud created by some uses of the verb *to be*. Strunk and White provide a nifty example. "There were leaves all over the ground" becomes "Leaves covered the ground." A four-word sentence outworks seven words.

In graduate school, Don Fry helped me see how my prose wilted under the weight of passive and *to be* verbs. Sentence after sentence, paragraph after paragraph began, "It is interesting to note that," or, "There are those occasions when" — pompous indirections bred by the quest for an advanced degree.

But there are sweet uses of *to be*, as Diane Ackerman demonstrates in defining one difference between men and women:

> The purpose of ritual for men *is* to learn the rules of power and competition. . . . The purpose of ritual for women . . . *is* to learn how to make human connections. They *are* often more intimate and vulnerable with one another than they *are* with their men, and taking care of other women teaches them to take care of themselves. In these formal ways, men and women domesticate their emotional lives. But their strategies *are* different, their biological itineraries *are* different. His sperm needs to travel, her egg needs to settle down. *It's* astonishing that they survive happily at all. (from *A Natural History of Love*)

"Domesticate" is a strong active verb. So is "needs" in the sentence about sperm and egg. But, mostly, the author uses the verb *to be*, what we once called — promiscuously — the copulative verb, to forge some daring intellectual connections.

Here, then, are your tools of thumb:

- Active verbs move the action and reveal the actors.
- Passive verbs emphasize the receiver, the victim.
- The verb *to be* links word and ideas.

These choices are not merely aesthetic. They can also be moral and political. In his essay "Politics and the English Language," George Orwell describes the relationship between language abuse and political abuse, how corrupt leaders use the passive voice to obscure unspeakable truths and shroud responsibility for their actions. They say, "It must be admitted, now that the report has been reviewed, that mistakes were made," rather than, "I read the report, and I admit I made a mistake." Here's a life tool: always apologize in the active voice.

## WORKSHOP

1. Read Orwell's "Politics and the English Language," and discuss his argument that the use of the passive voice contributes to the defense of the indefensible. As you listen to political speech, notice those occasions when politicians and other leaders use the passive voice to avoid responsibility for problems and mistakes.

2. Look for brilliant uses of the passive voice in the newspaper and in fiction. Conduct an imaginary debate with George Orwell in which you defend the passive.

3. Revise your passive and *to be* verbs into the active, and notice how the emphases in your sentences change. Pay attention to the changed connections — the cohesion — between one sentence and another. What additional revisions do these changes require?

4. The poet Donald Hall argues that active verbs can be too active, that they can lead to macho prose ("He crunched his fist into the Nazi's jaw") and cloying romanticism ("The horizon embraced the setting sun"). In your reading, look for examples of such overheated prose and imagine useful revisions.

# Tool 5

◄o►

# Watch those adverbs.

*Use them to change the meaning of the verb.*

The authors of the classic Tom Swift adventures for boys loved the exclamation point and the adverb. Consider this brief passage from *Tom Swift and His Great Searchlight:*

> "Look!" suddenly exclaimed Ned. "There's the agent now! . . . I'm going to speak to him!" impulsively declared Ned.

The exclamation point after "Look" should suffice to fire up the young reader, but the author adds "suddenly" and "exclaimed" for good measure. Time and again, the writer uses the adverb, not to change our understanding of the verb, but to intensify it. The silliness of this style led to a form of pun called the "Tom Swiftie," in which the adverb conveys the punch line:

> "I'm an artist," he said easily.
> "I need some pizza now," he said crustily.
> "I'm the Venus de Milo," she said disarmingly.
> "I dropped my toothpaste," he said, crestfallen.

At their best, adverbs spice up a verb or adjective. At their worst, they express a meaning already contained in it:

The blast *completely* destroyed the church office.
The cheerleader gyrated *wildly* before the screaming fans.
The accident *totally* severed the boy's arm.
The spy peered *furtively* through the bushes.

Consider the effect of deleting the adverbs:

The blast destroyed the church office.
The cheerleader gyrated before the screaming fans.
The accident severed the boy's arm.
The spy peered through the bushes.

In each case, the deletion shortens the sentence, sharpens the point, and creates elbow room for the verb. Feel free to disagree.

A half-century after his death, Meyer Berger remains among the greatest stylists in the history of the *New York Times*. One of his last columns describes the care received in a Catholic hospital by an old blind violinist:

> The staff talked with Sister Mary Fintan, who has charge of the hospital. With her consent they brought the old violin to Room 203. It had not been played for years, but Laurence Stroetz groped for it. His long white fingers stroked it. He tuned it, with some effort, and tightened the old bow. He lifted it to his chin and the lion's mane came down.

The vigor of verbs and the absence of adverbs mark Berger's prose. As the old man played "Ave Maria":

> Black-clad and white-clad nuns moved lips in silent prayer. They choked up. The long years on the Bowery had not stolen Laurence Stroetz's touch. Blindness made his fingers stumble down to the violin bridge, but they recovered. The music died and the audience pattered applause. The old violinist bowed and his sunken cheeks creased in a smile.

How much better that "the audience pattered applause" than that it "applauded politely."

Adverbiage reflects the style of an immature writer, but the masters can bump their shins as well. In 1963 John Updike wrote a one-paragraph essay, "Beer Can," about the beauty of that sacred vessel before the invention of the pop-top. He reminisced about how suds once "foamed eagerly in the exultation of release." As I've read that sentence over the years, I've grown more impatient with "eagerly." It clogs the space between a great verb ("foamed") and a great noun ("exultation"), which personify the beer and tell us all we need to know about eagerness.

To understand the difference between a good adverb and a bad adverb, consider these two sentences: "She smiled happily" and "She smiled sadly." Which one works best? The first seems weak because "smiled" contains the meaning of "happily." On the other hand, "sadly" changes the meaning.

Author Kurt Vonnegut uses adverbs with the frequency of an appearance of Halley's comet. I had to read several pages of his book *Palm Sunday* before I found one. Invited to deliver a Sunday sermon, he concludes the homily, "I thank you for your sweetly faked attention." Once again, "sweetly" adjusts the meaning of "faked." Good adverb.

Remember the song "Killing Me Softly"? Good adverb. How about "Killing Me Fiercely"? Bad adverb.

Look also for weak verb-adverb combinations that you can revise with stronger verbs: "She went quickly down the stairs" can become "She dashed down the stairs." "He listened surreptitiously" can become "He eavesdropped." Give yourself a choice.

I conclude with a disclaimer: The wealthiest writer in the world is J. K. Rowling, author of the Harry Potter series. She loves adverbs, especially when describing speech. On two pages of her first book, I found these attributions:

"said Hermione timidly."
"said Hermione faintly."

"he said simply."
"said Hagrid grumpily."
"said Hagrid irritably."

If you want to make more money than the Queen of England, maybe you should use more adverbs. If your aspirations, like mine, are more modest, use them sparingly.

## WORKSHOP

1. Look through the newspaper for any word that ends with -*ly*. If it's an adverb, cross it out and read the new sentence aloud. Which version works better?

2. Do the same for your last three pieces of writing. Circle the adverbs, delete them, and decide if the new sentence is stronger or weaker.

3. Read through your adverbs again and mark those that modify the verb rather than intensify it.

4. Search for weak verb-adverb combinations. "He spoke softly" might become "He whispered" or "He mumbled." If you come upon a weak combination, try a stronger verb to see if it improves the sentence.

◄○►

# Take it easy on the -*ings*.

*Prefer the simple present or past.*

An editor from *Newsday* told me the story of how he tried to help a reporter revise the top of a story. As often happens, the editor knew that the lead paragraph could be improved, but not how. As he walked down the hallway, story in hand, he looked up to see the Brobdingnagian figure of Jimmy Breslin, who agreed to take a peek at the problem.

"Too many -*ings*," said the legendary columnist.
"Too many whats?"
"Too many -*ings*."

Can a writer use too many words that end with -*ing*, and why should that be a problem?

To put it another way, why is "Wish and hope and think and pray" stronger than "Wishin' and hopin' and thinkin' and prayin' "? With apologies to Dusty Springfield, the answer resides in the history of English as an inflected language. An *inflection* is an element we add to a word to change its meaning. For example, we add -*s* or -*es* to a noun to indicate the plural. Add -*s* or -*ed* to a verb, and we distinguish present action from the past.

Add -*ing* to a verb, and it takes on a progressive sense —

a happening, as in this 1935 description by Richard Wright of the wild celebration after a Joe Louis boxing victory (the emphasis is mine): "Then they began *stopping* street cars. Like a cyclone *sweeping* through a forest, they went through them, *shouting, stamping.*" The passage survives the weak verb "went through," depending on a simile and those *-ing* words to create a sense of spontaneous action.

Consider this opening to the mystery novel *The Big Sleep:*

> It was about eleven o'clock in the morning, mid October, with the sun not *shining* and a look of hard wet rain in the clearness of the foothills. I was *wearing* my powder-blue suit, with dark blue shirt, tie and display handkerchief, black brogues, black wool socks with dark blue clocks on them. I was neat, clean, shaved and sober, and I didn't care who knew it. I was everything the well-dressed private detective ought to be. I was *calling* on four million dollars.

Even though author Raymond Chandler uses the static "was" five times, he creates a sense of the present — the here and now — by the injection of *-ing* words.

So the writer should not worry about the occasional and strategic use of an *-ing* word, only its overuse when the simple present or past tense will suffice. Sometimes a single *-ing* creates the desired effect. In this passage from a biography of U.S. Senator Bob Dole, we learn of the care he received after a terrible war injury:

> Bob held on, and made it through the operation. The fever disappeared and the other kidney worked, and by fall, they'd chipped away the whole cast. Now they *were trying* to get him out of bed. They hung his legs over the edge of the mattress, but it made him weak with fatigue. It took days to get him on his legs, and then he shook so, with the pain and the strangeness, they had to set him back in bed.

Using the simple past tense, Richard Ben Cramer creates a scene that is vivid, clear, and dramatic. There, in the middle, rests a single exception ("they were trying") to describe immediate and continuous effort.

Let me attempt to write a paragraph with too many -*ings:*

> *Suffering* under the strain of months of *withering* attacks, reservists stationed in Iraq are *complaining* to family members about the length of their tours of duty, and *lobbying* their congressional representatives about *bringing* more troops home soon.

There is nothing right or wrong about this sentence. It's just heavy on -*ings*, five of them, expressing a variety of syntactic forms:

- "Suffering" is a present participle, modifying "reservists."
- "Withering" is an adjective, modifying "attacks."
- "Complaining" and "lobbying" are progressive forms of verbs.
- "Bringing" is a gerund, a verb used as a noun.

Before I try to improve this passage, let me offer two reasons why -*ing* weakens a verb:

1. When I add -*ing*, I add a syllable to the word, which does not happen, in most cases, when I add -*s* or -*ed*. Let's take the verb *to trick*. First, I'll add -*s*, then -*ed*, giving me *tricks* and *tricked*. Neither change alters the root effect of the verb. *Tricking*, with its extra syllable, sounds like a different word.

2. The -*ing* words begin to resemble each other. Walking and running and cycling and swimming are all good forms of exercise, but I prefer to point out that my friend Kelly likes to walk, run, cycle, and swim.

What might a revised version of my Iraq passage look like? How about:

> Reservists stationed in Iraq have suffered months of withering attacks. They have complained to family members about the lengths of their tours of duty and lobbied Congress to bring more troops home soon.

I cannot argue that this revision represents a significant improvement over the earlier version; it's perhaps a little cleaner and more direct. But now I know that this tool gives me choices I did not know I had. In the same way I test adverbs, I can now test my *-ings*.

Since I've learned this tool, I notice how I appreciate passages that are *-ing* lite. Listen to Kathleen Norris in *Dakota:*

> Like many who have written about Dakota, I'm invigorated by the harsh beauty of the land and feel a need to tell the stories that come from its soil. *Writing* is a solitary act, and ideally, the Dakotas might seem to provide a writer with ample solitude and quiet. But the frantic social activity in small towns conspires to silence a person. There are far fewer people than jobs to fill. Someone must be found to lead the church choir or youth group, to bowl with the league, to coach a softball team or little league, to run a Chamber of Commerce or club committee. Many jobs are vital: the volunteer fire department and ambulance service, the domestic violence hotline, the food pantry. All too often a kind of Tom Sawyerism takes over, and makes of adult life a perpetual club. Imagine *spending* the rest of your life at summer camp.

In a paragraph of 151 words, Norris gives us only two *-ings*. Not too many.

## WORKSHOP

1. Read your recent work. Circle any word that ends with *-ing*. What have you discovered? Do you use too many *-ings*?

2. If so, revise a few passages. See if you can knock off some -*ings*, using, instead, the simple present or past.

3. Notice the number of -*ings* in the work you admire.

4. If you come across a difficult passage to read or write, test it for -*ings*.

# TOOL 7

-◄O►-

# Fear not the long sentence.

*Take the reader on a journey
of language and meaning.*

Everyone fears the long sentence. Editors fear it. Readers fear it.
Most of all, writers fear it. Even I fear it. Look. Another short one.
Shorter. Fragments. Frags. Just letters. F . . . f . . . f . . . f. Can I
write a sentence without words? Just punctuation? . . . #:!?

Write what you fear. Until the writer tries to master the long
sentence, she is no writer at all, for while length makes a bad sentence worse, it can make a good sentence better.

My favorite Tom Wolfe essay from the early days of the New
Journalism movement is "A Sunday Kind of Love," named after a
romantic ballad of the period. The events described take place
one morning in a New York subway station on a Thursday, not a
Sunday. Wolfe sees and seizes a moment of youthful passion on
the city underground to redefine urban romance.

> Love! Attar of libido in the air! It is 8:45 A.M. Thursday morning
> in the IRT subway station at 50th Street and Broadway and al-
> ready two kids are hung up in a kind of herringbone weave of
> arms and legs, which proves, one has to admit, that love is not
> *confined* to Sunday in New York.

That's a fine beginning. Erotic fragments and exclamation points. The concave/convex connection of love captured in "herringbone weave," the quick movement from short sentence to long, as writer and reader dive from the top of the ladder of abstraction, from love and libido, down to two kids making out, back up to variations on amour in the metropolis.

During rush hour, subway travelers learn the meaning of *length:* the length of the platform, the length of the wait, the length of the train, the length of the escalators and stairwells to ground level, the length of lines of hurried, grouchy, impatient commuters. Notice how Wolfe uses the length of his sentences to reflect that reality:

> Still the odds! All the faces come popping in clots out of the Seventh Avenue local, past the King Size Ice Cream machine, and the turnstiles start whacking away as if the world were breaking up on the reefs. Four steps past the turnstiles everybody is already backed up haunch to paunch for the climb up the ramp and the stairs to the surface, a great funnel of flesh, wool, felt, leather, rubber and steaming alumicron, with the blood squeezing through everybody's old sclerotic arteries in hopped-up spurts from too much coffee and the effort of surfacing from the subway at the rush hour. Yet there on the landing are a boy and a girl, both about eighteen, in one of those utter, My Sin, backbreaking embraces.

This is classic Wolfe, a world where "sclerotic" serves as antonym for *erotic,* where exclamation points sprout like wildflowers, where experience and status are defined by brand names. ("My Sin" was a perfume of the day.) But wait! There's more! As the couple canoodles, a cavalcade of commuters passes by:

> All round them, ten, scores, it seems like hundreds, of faces and bodies are perspiring, trooping and bellying up the stairs with arterio-sclerotic grimaces past a showcase full of such novel items

as Joy Buzzers, Squirting Nickels, Finger Rats, Scary Tarantulas and spoons with realistic dead flies on them, past Fred's barbershop, which is just off the landing and has glossy photographs of young men with the kind of baroque haircuts one can get in there, and up onto 50th Street into a madhouse of traffic and shops with weird lingerie and gray hair-dyeing displays in the windows, signs for free teacup readings and a pool-playing match between the Playboy Bunnies and Downey's Showgirls, and then everybody pounds on toward the Time-Life Building, the Brill Building or NBC.

Has any reader ever experienced a more glorious long sentence, a more rollicking evocation of underground New York, a more dazzling 128 words from capital letter to period? If you find one, I'd like to read it.

A close reading of Wolfe suggests some strategies to achieve mastery of the long sentence:

- It helps if subject and verb of the main clause come early in the sentence.
- Use the long sentence to describe something long. Let form follow function.
- It helps if the long sentence is written in chronological order.
- Use the long sentence in variation with sentences of short and medium length.
- Use the long sentence as a list or catalog of products, names, images.
- Long sentences need more editing than short ones. Make every word count. Even. In. A. Very. Long. Sentence.

Writing long sentences means going against the grain. But isn't that what the best writers do? In his novel *The Rings of Saturn*, W. G. Sebald uses the long sentence to explain — and mirror — the antique prose style of English essayist Sir Thomas Browne:

In common with other English writers of the seventeenth century, Browne wrote out of the fullness of his erudition, deploying a vast repertoire of quotations and the names of authorities who had gone before, creating complex metaphors and analogies, and constructing labyrinthine sentences that sometimes extend over one or two pages, sentences that resemble processions or a funeral cortege in their sheer ceremonial lavishness. It is true that, because of the immense weight of the impediments he is carrying, Browne's writing can be held back by the force of gravitation, but when he does succeed in rising higher and higher through the circles of his spiralling prose, borne aloft like a glider on warm currents of air, even today the reader is overcome by a sense of levitation.

In the 1940s Rudolf Flesch described the effects that made a sentence "easy" or "hard" to read. According to Flesch, an 1893 study illuminated the shrinking English sentence: "The average Elizabethan written sentence ran to about 45 words; the Victorian sentence to 29; ours to 20 and less." Flesch used sentence length and syllable count as factors in his readability studies, an arithmetic once derided by E. B. White in his essay "Calculating Machine." "Writing is an act of faith," wrote White, "not a trick of grammar."

The good writer must believe that a good sentence, short or long, will not be lost on the reader. And although Flesch preached the value of the good eighteen-word sentence, he praised long sentences written by such masters as Joseph Conrad. So even for old Rudolf, a long sentence, well crafted, was not a sin against the Flesch.

## WORKSHOP

1. Keep an eye out for well-crafted long sentences. Test them in context, using the criteria above.

2. During revision, most journalists take a longish sentence and break it up for clarity. But writers also learn to combine sen-

tences for good effect. Review examples of your recent work. Combine shorter sentences for a richer variety of sentence structures and lengths.

3. Here's a passage from the novel *The Diving Bell and the Butterfly* by Jean-Dominique Bauby:

> I am fading away. Slowly but surely. Like the sailor who watches the home shore gradually disappear, I watch my past recede. My old life still burns within me, but more and more of it is reduced to the ashes of memory.

Revise this excerpt into a single sentence.

4. The best long sentences flow from good research and reporting. Review Wolfe's sentences above. Notice the details that come from direct observation and note taking. The next time you report in the field, look for scenes and settings that lend themselves to description in a long sentence.

5. Sentences can be divided into four structural categories: simple (one clause); complex (main clause plus dependent clauses); compound (more than one main clause); compound-complex. But a long sentence does not have to be compound or complex. It can be simple:

> A tornado ripped through St. Petersburg Friday, tearing roofs off dozens of houses, shattering glass windows of downtown businesses, uprooting palm trees near bayside parks, and leaving Clyde Howard cowering in his claw-footed bathtub.

That thirty-four-word sentence is a simple sentence with one main clause ("A tornado ripped"). In this case the -*ings* help. Survey the contents of your purse, your wallet, or a favorite junk drawer. Write a long simple sentence to describe what's inside.

# TOOL 8

◄o►

# Establish a pattern, then give it a twist.

*Build parallel constructions,*
*but cut across the grain.*

Writers shape up their prose by building parallel structures in their words, phrases, and sentences. "If two or more ideas are parallel," writes Diana Hacker in *A Writer's Reference*, "they are easier to grasp when expressed in parallel grammatical form. Single words should be balanced with single words, phrases with phrases, clauses with clauses."

The effect is most obvious in the words of great orators, such as Martin Luther King Jr. (the emphasis is mine):

> So let freedom ring from the *prodigious hilltops* of New Hampshire. Let freedom ring from the *mighty mountains* of New York. Let freedom ring from the *heightening Alleghenies* of Pennsylvania! Let freedom ring from the *snowcapped Rockies* of Colorado.

Notice how King builds a crescendo from the repetition of words and grammatical structures, in this case a series of prepositional phrases with a noun designating mountains and an adjective defining majesty.

"Use parallels wherever you can," wrote Sheridan Baker in *The Practical Stylist*, "equivalent thoughts demand parallel constructions." Just after reading Baker, I stumbled on an essay by one of my favorite English authors, G. K. Chesterton, who wrote detective stories, books on religion, and literary essays early in the twentieth century. His more mannered style highlights the parallel structures in his sentences: "With *my* stick and *my* knife, *my* chalks and *my* brown paper, I went out on to the great downs." That sentence strides across the page on the legs of two parallel constructions: the fourfold repetition of "my," and the pair of pairs connected by "and."

The late Neil Postman argued that the problems of society could not be solved by information alone. He shaped his arguments around a set of parallel propositions:

> If there are people starving in the world — and there are — it is not caused by insufficient information. If crime is rampant in the streets, it is not caused by insufficient information. If children are abused and wives are battered, that has nothing to do with insufficient information. If our schools are not working and democratic principles are losing their force, that too has nothing to do with insufficient information. If we are plagued by such problems, it is because something else is missing.

By repeating those conditional "If" clauses and ending four consecutive sentences with "insufficient information," Postman sounds a drumbeat of language, a drumline of persuasion.

Suddenly I began to see parallels everywhere. Here is a passage from *The Plot Against America,* a novel by Philip Roth. In one of his trademark long sentences, Roth describes Jewish American working-class life in the 1940s:

> The men worked *fifty, sixty, even seventy* or more hours a week; the women worked all the time, with little assistance from labor-saving devices, *washing laundry,* ironing shirts, mending socks, turning collars, sewing on buttons, mothproofing woolens, polishing furniture, sweeping and washing floors, washing windows, *cleaning sinks, tubs, toilets, and stoves,* vacuuming rugs, nursing the sick, shopping for food, cooking meals, feeding relatives, tidy-

ing closets and drawers, overseeing paint jobs and household re-
pairs, arranging for religious observances, paying bills and keeping the family's books while simultaneously attending to their
children's health, clothing, cleanliness, schooling, nutrition, conduct, birthdays, discipline, and morale.

In this dazzling inventory of work, I count nineteen parallel
phrases, all building on "washing laundry." (And look at all those
*-ings.*) But here's Roth's secret: what makes the passage sing is the
occasional variation of the pattern, such as the phrase "cleaning
sinks, tubs, toilets, and stoves." Roth could have written, "The
men worked fifty, sixty, seventy hours a week," a perfectly parallel
string of adjectives. Instead, he gives us "even seventy or more."
By breaking the pattern, he lends more emphasis to the final
element.

A pure parallel construction would be "Boom, boom,
boom." Parallelism with a twist gives us "Boom, boom, bang."
A pattern with variation created these now familiar phrases and
titles:

Hither, thither, and yon
Wynken, Blynken, and Nod
Father, Son, and Holy Ghost
Peter, Paul, and Mary
Sex, drugs, and rock 'n' roll

Superman, we all remember, stands not for truth, justice, and pa-
triotism, but "truth, justice, and the American way," two parallel
nouns with a twist.

Such intentional violation of parallelism adds power to the
conclusion of King's speech:

Let freedom ring from the *curvaceous peaks* of California! [That
follows the pattern.] But not only that; let freedom ring from
*Stone Mountain* of Georgia!

Let freedom ring from *Lookout Mountain* of Tennessee! Let freedom ring from *every hill and molehill* of Mississippi. From every
mountainside, let freedom ring.

When King points the compass of freedom toward the segre-
gationist South, he alters the pattern. Generalized American to-
pography is replaced by specific locations associated with racial
injustice: Stone Mountain and Lookout Mountain. The final
variation covers not just mighty mountains, but every bump of
Mississippi.

All writers fail, on occasion, to take advantage of parallel
structures. The result for the reader can be the equivalent of driving over a pothole on a freeway. What if Saint Paul taught us that
the three great virtues were faith, hope, and committing ourselves to charitable work? What if Abraham Lincoln had written
about a government of the people, by the people, and for the entire nation, including the red and blue states? These violations of
parallelism should remind us of the exquisite balance of the original versions.

## WORKSHOP

1. Examine your recent work with parallelism in mind. Look
for examples in which you used parallel structures. Can you find
potholes — some unparallel phrases or sentences — that jar the
reader?

2. Notice parallel language in novels, in creative nonfiction,
in journalism. When you find a passage, underline the parallel
structures with a pencil. Discuss the effects of parallelism on the
reader.

3. Just for fun, take parallel slogans or sayings and rewrite the
last element. For example, John, Paul, George, and that drummer
who wears the rings.

4. By fiddling with parallel structures, you might discover
that an occasional violation of parallelism — a twist at the end —
can lend a humorous imbalance to a sentence. Give it a try.

# Let punctuation control pace and space.

*Learn the rules, but realize*
*you have more options than you think.*

Some teach punctuation using technical distinctions, such as the difference between restrictive and nonrestrictive clauses. Not here. I prefer tools, not rules. My preference shows no disrespect for the rules of punctuation. They help the writer and the reader as long as everyone remembers that such rules are arbitrary, determined by consensus, convention, and culture.

If you check the end of that last sentence, you will notice that I used a comma before "and" to end a series. For a quarter century, we at the Poynter Institute have argued about that comma. Fans of Strunk and White (that's me!) put it in. Thrifty journalists take it out. As an American, I spell the word *color* "color," and I place the comma inside the quotation marks. My cheeky English friend spells it "colour", and she leaves that poor little croissant out in the cold.

Most punctuation is required, but some is optional, leaving the writer with many choices. My modest goal is to highlight those choices, to transform the formal rules of punctuation into useful tools.

*Punctuation* comes from the Latin root *punctus,* or "point." Those funny dots, lines, and squiggles help writers point the way. To help readers, we punctuate for two reasons:

1. To set the pace of reading.
2. To divide words, phrases, and ideas into convenient groupings.

You will punctuate with power and purpose when you begin to consider pace and space.

Think of a long, well-written sentence with no punctuation except the period. Such a sentence is a straight road with a stop sign at the end. The period is the stop sign. Now think of a winding road with lots of stop signs. That analogy describes a paragraph with lots of periods, an effect that will slow the pace of the story. The writer may desire such a pace for strategic reasons: to achieve clarity, convey emotion, or create suspense.

If a period is a stop sign, then what kind of traffic flow is created by other marks? The comma is a speed bump; the semicolon is what a driver education teacher calls a "rolling stop"; the parenthetical expression is a detour; the colon is a flashing yellow light that announces something important up ahead; the dash is a tree branch in the road.

A writer once told me that he knew it was time to hand in a story when he had reached this stage: "I would take out all the commas. Then I would put them all back." The comma may be the most versatile of marks and the one most closely associated with the writer's voice. A well-placed comma points to where the writer would pause if he read the passage aloud. "He may have been a genius, as mutations sometimes are." The author of that line is Kurt Vonnegut. I have heard him speak, and that central comma *is* his voice.

More muscular than the comma, the semicolon is most useful for dividing and organizing big chunks of information. In his essay "The Lantern-Bearers," Robert Louis Stevenson describes an adventure game in which boys wore cheap tin lanterns — called *bull's-eyes* — under their coats:

> We wore them buckled to the waist upon a cricket belt, and over them, such was the rigour of the game, a buttoned top-coat. They

smelled noisomely of blistered tin; they never burned aright, though they would always burn our fingers; their use was naught; the pleasure of them merely fanciful; and yet a boy with a bull's-eye under his top-coat asked for nothing more.

Parentheses introduce a play within a play. Like a detour sign in the middle of a street, they require the driver to maneuver around to regain the original direction. Parenthetical expressions are best kept short and (Pray for us, Saint Nora of Ephron) witty.

My great friend Don Fry has undertaken a quixotic quest to eliminate that tree branch in the road — the dash. "Avoid the dash," he insists as often as William Strunk begged his students to "omit needless words." Don's crusade was inspired by his observation — with which I agree — that the dash has become the default mark for writers who never mastered the formal rules. But the dash has two brilliant uses: a pair of dashes can set off an idea contained within a sentence, and a dash near the end can deliver a punch line.

In his book *Propaganda*, Edward Bernays uses both kinds of dashes to describe the purposes of political persuasion:

> Propaganda does exist on all sides of us, and it does change our mental pictures of the world. Even if this be unduly pessimistic — and that remains to be proved — the opinion reflects a tendency that is undoubtedly real.
>
> We are proud of our diminishing infant death rate — and that too is the work of propaganda.

That leaves the colon, and here's what it does: it announces a word, phrase, or clause the way a trumpet flourish in a Shakespeare play sounds the arrival of the royal procession. More from Vonnegut:

> I am often asked to give advice to young writers who wish to be famous and fabulously well-to-do. This is the best I have to offer:

While looking as much like a bloodhound as possible, announce that you are working twelve hours a day on a masterpiece. Warning: All is lost if you crack a smile. (from *Palm Sunday*)

Writers store other punctuation arrows in their quiver, including ellipses, brackets, exclamation points, and capital letters. These have formal uses, of course, but in the hands of an inventive writer they can express all the organ stops of voice, pitch, and tone. Here, for example, James McBride describes the power of a preacher in *The Color of Water*:

"We . . . [silence] . . . know . . . today . . . arrhh . . . um . . . I said WEEEE . . . know . . . THAT [silence] ahhh . . . JESUS [church: "Amen!"] . . . ahhh, CAME DOWN . . . ["Yes! Amen!"] I said CAME DOWWWWNNNN! ["Go on!"] He CAME-ON-DOWN-AND — LED-THE — PEOPLE-OF — JERU-SALEM-AMEN!"

When it comes to punctuation, all writers develop habits that buttress their styles. Mine include wearing out the comma and using more periods than average. I abhor unsightly blemishes, so I shun semicolons and parentheses. I overuse the colon. I write an exclamation with enough force to avoid the weedy appendage of an exclamation point. I prefer the comma to the dash but sometimes use one — if only to pluck Don Fry's beard.

## WORKSHOP

1. Make sure you have a good basic reference to guide you through the rules of punctuation. I favor *A Writer's Reference* by Diana Hacker. For fun, read *Eats, Shoots & Leaves*, a humorous if crusty attack by Lynne Truss against faulty punctuation, especially in public texts.

2. Take one of your old pieces and repunctuate it. Add some optional commas, or take some out. Read both versions aloud. Hear a difference?

3. Make conscious decisions on how fast you'd like the reader to move. Perhaps you want readers to zoom across the landscape. Or to tiptoe through a technical explanation. Punctuate accordingly.

4. Reread this section and analyze my use of punctuation. Challenge my choices. Repunctuate it.

5. When you gain confidence, have some fun and use the punctuation marks described above as well as ellipses, brackets, and capital letters. Take inspiration from the passage by James McBride.

◄○►

# Cut big, then small.

*Prune the big limbs, then shake out the dead leaves.*

When writers fall in love with their words, it is a good feeling that can lead to a bad effect. When we fall in love with all our quotes, characters, anecdotes, and metaphors, we cannot bear to kill any of them. But kill we must. In 1914 British author Arthur Quiller-Couch wrote it bluntly: "Murder your darlings."

Such ruthlessness is best applied at the end of the process, when creativity can be moderated by coldhearted judgment. A fierce discipline must make every word count.

"Vigorous writing is concise," wrote William Strunk in the first edition of *The Elements of Style.*

> A sentence should contain no unnecessary words, a paragraph no unnecessary sentences, for the same reason that a drawing should have no unnecessary lines and a machine no unnecessary parts. This requires not that the writer make all his sentences short, or that he avoid all detail and treat his subjects only in outline, but that he make every word tell.

But how to do that?

Begin by cutting the big stuff. Donald Murray taught me that brevity comes from selection, not compression, a lesson that requires lifting blocks from the work. When Maxwell Perkins edited Thomas Wolfe, he confronted manuscripts that could be weighed by the pound and delivered in a wheelbarrow. The famous editor once advised the famous author: "It does not seem to me that the book is over-written. Whatever comes out of it must come out block by block and not sentence by sentence." Perkins reduced one four-page passage about Wolfe's uncle to six words: "Henry, the oldest, was now thirty."

If your goal is to achieve precision and concision, begin by pruning the big limbs. You can shake out the dead leaves later.

- Cut any passage that does not support your focus.
- Cut the weakest quotations, anecdotes, and scenes to give greater power to the strongest.
- Cut any passage you have written to satisfy a tough teacher or editor rather than the common reader.
- Don't invite others to cut. You know the work better. Mark optional trims. Then decide whether they should become actual cuts.

Always leave time for revision, but if pressed, shoot for a draft and a half. That means cutting phrases, words, even syllables in a hurry. The paradigm for such word editing is the work of William Zinsser. In the second chapter of *On Writing Well*, he demonstrates how he cut the clutter from final drafts of his own book. "Although they look like a first draft, they had already been rewritten and retyped . . . four or five times. With each rewrite I try to make what I have written tighter, stronger and more precise, eliminating every element that is not doing useful work."

In his draft, Zinsser writes of the struggling reader: "My sympathies are entirely with him. He's not so dumb. If the reader is lost, it is generally because the writer of the article has not been careful enough to keep him on the proper path." That passage seems lean enough, so it's instructive to watch the author cut the fat. In his revision "entirely" gets the knife. So does "He's not so dumb." So does "of the article." And so does "proper." (I confess that I would keep "proper path," just for the alliteration. But "path" contains the meaning of "proper.")

The revised passage: "My sympathies are with him. If the reader is lost, it is generally because the writer has not been careful enough to keep him on the path." Twenty-seven words outwork the original thirty-six.

Targets for cuts include:

- Adverbs that intensify rather than modify: *just, certainly, entirely, extremely, completely, exactly.*
- Prepositional phrases that repeat the obvious: *in the story, in the article, in the movie, in the city.*
- Phrases that grow on verbs: *seems to, tends to, should have to, tries to.*
- Abstract nouns that hide active verbs: *consideration* becomes *considers; judgment* becomes *judges; observation* becomes *observes.*
- Restatements: *a sultry, humid afternoon.*

The previous draft of this essay contained 850 words (see below). This version contains 678, a savings of 20 percent.

## TOOL 10: PREVIOUS DRAFT

When writers fall in love with their words, it is a good ~~and power-ful~~ feeling that can lead to a bad ~~and dangerous~~ effect. ~~Jacqui Banaszynski reaches a point where she feels so immersed in her work that every reflection, conversation, observation seems connected to her writing passion. She calls this "being in full story."~~ When we fall in love with all our quotes, ~~all our~~ characters, ~~all our~~ anecdotes, ~~all our~~ *and* metaphors, ~~it seems impossible for us~~ we cannot bear to kill any of them. But kill we must. In 1914 British author Arthur Quiller-Couch ~~put it more~~ wrote it bluntly: "Murder your darlings."

Such ruthlessness is best applied at the end of the process, where ~~the free flow of~~ creativity can be ~~replaced~~ moderated by cold-hearted judgment. ~~To become a card-carrying member of Chip Scanlan's Word Cutting Club,~~ A fierce discipline ~~and cleared-eyed evaluation~~ must make every word count.

"Vigorous writing is concise," wrote William Strunk ~~when~~ *in the first edition of The Elements of Style.* ~~E.B. White was still his student.~~

"A sentence should contain no unnecessary words, a paragraph no unnecessary sentences, for the same reason that a drawing should have no unnecessary lines and a machine no unnecessary parts. This requires not that the writer make all his sentences short, or that he avoid all detail and treat his subjects only in outline, but that he make every word tell."

But how to do that? *Donald Murray taught me*
Begin by cutting the big stuff. ~~It is hard to learn~~ that brevity comes from selection, not compression," a lesson that requires lifting ~~whole parts~~ blocks from the work. When Maxwell Perkins edited ~~the work of~~ Thomas Wolfe, he ~~often~~ confronted manuscripts that could be ~~measured~~ *weighed* by the pound and delivered in a wheelbarrow. The famous editor once advised the famous author: "It does not seem to me that the book is over-written. Whatever comes out of it must come out block by block and not

sentence by sentence." ~~One~~ **Perkins reduced** ~~One~~ four-page passage about Wolfe's uncle ~~was reduced~~ to six words: "Henry, the oldest, was now thirty."

If your goal is to achieve ~~concision and precision~~ precision and concision, begin by pruning the big limbs. You can shake out the dead leaves later.

- Cut ~~out~~ any passage that does not support ~~the focus or central theme of the story~~ your focus.
- ~~If you have a number of~~ Cut the weakest quotations, anecdotes, **and** ~~or~~ scenes ~~that sharpen the point of the story, cut the weakest of these, which will~~ to give greater power to the strongest.
- Cut ~~out~~ any passage you have written ~~to avoid prosecutorial editing or to satisfy what you think will be a teacher's requirements~~ **to** satisfy a tough teacher or editor, rather than the common reader.
- Don't invite others to cut ~~based on their judgment.~~ You know the work better. Mark "optional trims." ~~Now ask yourself~~ **Then decide** ~~whether these options.~~ **whether** [Should] [they] become actual cut[s].

~~Even if you don't have time for much revision,~~ Always leave time for revision, but if you are pressed, shoot for a draft and a half. That means cutting phrases, words, even syllables in a hurry. The ~~greatest model for this kind of revision~~ paradigm for such word editing is the work of William Zinsser. ~~Take a look at~~ In the second chapter of *On Writing Well,* he demonstrates how he cut the clutter ~~out of manuscript pages~~ from final drafts of his own book. "Although they look like a first draft, they had already been rewritten and retyped|.|.|. four or five times. With each rewrite I try to make what I have written tighter, stronger and more precise, eliminating every element that is not doing useful work."

In his draft, Zinsser writes of the struggling reader: "My sympathies are entirely with him. He's not so dumb. If the reader is lost, it is generally because the writer of the article has not been careful enough to keep him on the proper path." That passage seems lean enough ~~to me~~, so it's instructive to watch the author ~~zero in on the weakest words slice~~ the fat. In his revision "entirely" gets the knife. So does "He's not so dumb." So does "of the article." And so does "proper." (I confess that I would keep "proper path," just for the alliteration. ~~Keeping you on the~~ But "path" contains the meaning of "proper.")

The revised passage: "My sympathies are with him. If the reader is lost, it is generally because the writer has not been careful enough to keep him on the path." Twenty-seven words outwork the original ~~66, a savings of 25 percent~~.

~~Here are some targets for cuts. Look for.~~ Targets for cuts include:

- ~~Look for~~ Adverbs that intensify rather than modify ~~the meaning~~: just, certainly, entirely, extremely, completely, exactly.
- ~~Look for~~ Prepositional phrases that repeat the obvious: in the story, in the article, in the movie, in the city.
- ~~Look for~~ Phrases that grow on verbs: seems to, tends to, should have to, tries to.
- ~~Look for~~ Abstract nouns that hide active verbs: consideration becomes considers; judgment becomes judges; observation becomes observes.
- Restatements: a sultry, humid afternoon.

## WORKSHOP

1. Compare and contrast my longer draft with my shorter one. Which revisions make the essay better? Have I cut something you would have retained? State your case for keeping it.

2. Get a copy of *On Writing Well*. Study the cuts Zinsser makes on pages 10 and 11. See if any patterns emerge. Hint: notice what he does with adverbs.

3. Watch a DVD version of a movie, and pay attention to the feature called *extra scenes*. Discuss with friends the director's decisions. Why was a particular scene left on the cutting room floor?

4. Now review your own work. Cut without mercy. Begin with big cuts, then small ones. Count how many words you've saved. Calculate the percentage of the whole. Can you cut 15 percent?

5. Flip open to a page of this book at random. Search for clutter. Cut words that do no work.

—◀○▶—

# PART TWO

# Special Effects

—◄o►—

# Prefer the simple over the technical.

*Use shorter words, sentences,*
*and paragraphs at points of complexity.*

This tool celebrates simplicity, but a clever writer can make the simple complex — and to good effect. This requires a literary technique called *defamiliarization*, a hopeless word that describes the process by which an author takes the familiar and makes it strange. Film directors create this effect with super close-ups and with shots from severe or distorting angles. More difficult to achieve on the page, this effect can dazzle the reader as does E. B. White's description of a humid day in Florida:

> On many days, the dampness of the air pervades all life, all living. Matches refuse to strike. The towel, hung to dry, grows wetter by the hour. The newspaper, with its headlines about integration, wilts in your hand and falls limply into the coffee and the egg. Envelopes seal themselves. Postage stamps mate with one another as shamelessly as grasshoppers. (from "The Ring of Time")

What could be more familiar than a mustache on a teacher's face, but not this mustache, as described by Roald Dahl in his childhood memoir, *Boy:*

A truly terrifying sight, a thick orange hedge that sprouted and flourished between his nose and his upper lip and ran clear across his face from the middle of one cheek to the middle of the other. ... [It] was curled most splendidly upwards all the way along as though it had had a permanent wave put into it or possibly curling tongs heated in the mornings over a tiny flame. ... The only other way he could have achieved this curling effect, we boys decided, was by prolonged upward brushing with a hard toothbrush in front of the looking-glass every morning.

Both White and Dahl take the common — the humid day and the mustache — and, through the filter of their prose styles, force us to see it in a new way.

More often, the writer must find a way to simplify prose in service to the reader. For balance, call the strategy *familiarization*, taking the strange or opaque or complex and, through the power of explanation, making it comprehensible, even familiar.

Too often, writers render complicated ideas with complicated prose, producing sentences such as this one, from an editorial about state government:

To avert the all too common enactment of requirements without regard for their local cost and tax impact, however, the commission recommends that statewide interest should be clearly identified on any proposed mandates, and that the state should partially reimburse local government for some state imposed mandates and fully for those involving employee compensation, working conditions and pensions.

The density of this passage has two possible explanations: The writer is writing, not for a general audience, but for a specialized one, legal experts already familiar with the issues. Or, the writer thinks that form should follow function, that complicated ideas should be communicated in complicated prose.

He needs the advice of writing coach Donald Murray, who

argues that the reader benefits from shorter words and phrases, and simpler sentences, at the points of greatest complexity. What would happen if readers encountered this translation of the editorial?

> The state of New York often passes laws telling local governments what to do. These laws have a name. They are called "state mandates." On many occasions, these laws improve life for everyone in the state. But they come with a cost. Too often, the state doesn't consider the cost to local government, or how much money taxpayers will have to shell out. So we have an idea. The state should pay back local governments for some of these so-called mandates.

The differences in these passages are worth measuring. The first one takes six and a half lines of text. The revision requires an additional half line. But consider this: The original writer has room for fifty-eight words in six and a half lines, while I get eighty-one words in seven lines, including fifty-nine one-syllable words. His six and a half lines give him room for only one sentence. I fit eight sentences into seven lines. My words and sentences are shorter. The passage is clearer. I use this strategy to fulfill a mission: to make the strange workings of government transparent to the average citizen, to make the strange familiar.

George Orwell reminds us to avoid long words where short ones "will do," a preference that exalts short Saxon words over longer ones of Greek and Latin origin, words that entered the language after the Norman Conquest in 1066. According to such a standard, *box* beats out *container; chew* trumps *masticate;* and *ragtop* outcools *convertible.*

I am often stunned by the power that authors generate with words of a single syllable, as in this passage from Amy Tan:

> The mother accepted this and closed her eyes. The sword came down and sliced back and forth, up and down, *whish! whish! whish!* And the mother screamed and shouted, cried out in terror

and pain. But when she opened her eyes, she saw no blood, no shredded flesh.

The girl said, "Do you see now?" (from *The Joy Luck Club*)

Fifty-five words in all, forty-eight of one syllable. Only one word ("accepted") of three syllables. Even the book title works this way.

Simple language can make hard facts easy reading. Consider the first paragraph of Dava Sobel's *Longitude:*

> Once on a Wednesday excursion when I was a little girl, my father bought me a beaded wire ball that I loved. At a touch, I could collapse the toy into a flat coil between my palms, or pop it open to make a hollow sphere. Rounded out, it resembled a tiny Earth, because its hinged wires traced the same pattern of intersecting circles that I had seen on the globe in my schoolroom — the thin black lines of latitude and longitude. The few colored beads slid along the wire paths haphazardly, like ships on the high seas.

Simplicity is not handed to the writer. It is the product of imagination and craft, a created effect.

Remember that clear prose is not just a product of sentence length and word choice. It derives first from a sense of purpose — a determination to inform. What comes next is the hard work of reporting, research, and critical thinking. The writer cannot make something clear until the difficult subject is clear in the writer's head. Then, and only then, does she reach into the writer's toolbox, ready to explain to readers, "Here's how it works."

## WORKSHOP

1. Review writing you think is unclear, dense with information. A tax form, perhaps, or a legal contract. Study the length of words, sentences, and paragraphs. What have you discovered?

2. Repeat the process with your prose. Pay attention to passages you now think are too complicated. Revise a passage using the tools described in this section.

3. Collect examples of stories where the writer has turned hard facts into easy reading. Start by browsing through a good academic encyclopedia.

4. Look for an opportunity to use the sentence "Here's how it works."

—◄o►—

# Give key words their space.

*Do not repeat a distinctive word
unless you intend a specific effect.*

I coined the phrase *word territory* to describe a tendency I notice in my own writing. When I read a story I wrote months or years ago, I am surprised by how often I repeat words without care. Writers may choose to repeat words or phrases for emphasis or rhythm: Abraham Lincoln was not redundant in his hope that "government of the people, by the people, for the people, shall not perish from the earth." Only a mischievous or tone-deaf editor would delete the repetition of "people."

To preserve word territory, you must recognize the difference between intended and unintended repetition. For example, I once wrote this sentence to describe a writing tool: "Long sentences *create* a flow that carries the reader down a stream of understanding, *creating* an effect that Don Fry calls 'steady advance.'" It took several years and hundreds of readings before I noticed I had written "create" and "creating" in the same sentence. It was easy enough to cut "creating," giving the stronger verb form its own space. Word territory.

In 1978 I wrote this ending to a story about the life and death of Beat writer Jack Kerouac in my hometown of St. Petersburg, Florida:

How fitting then that this child of *bliss* should come in the end to St. Petersburg. Our city of golden sunshine, balmy serenity and careless *bliss*, a paradise for those who have known hard times. And, at once, the city of wretched loneliness, the city of rootless survival and of restless wanderers, the city where so many come to die.

Years later, I admire that passage except for the unintended repetition of the key word "bliss." Worse yet, I had used it before, two paragraphs earlier. I offer no excuse other than feeling blissed out in the aura of Kerouac's work.

I've heard a story, which I cannot verify, that Ernest Hemingway tried to write book pages in which no key words were repeated. That effect would mark a hard-core adherence to word territory, but, in fact, does not reflect the way Hemingway writes. He often repeats key words on a page — *table, rock, fish, river, sea* — because to find a synonym strains the writer's eyes and the reader's ears.

Consider this passage from *A Moveable Feast* (the emphasis is mine):

> "All you have to do is write *one true sentence*. Write the *truest sentence* that you know." So finally I would write *one true sentence*, and then go on from there. It was easy then because there was always *one true sentence* that I knew or had seen or had heard someone say. If I started to write elaborately, or like someone introducing or presenting something, I found that I could cut that scrollwork or ornament out and throw it away and start with the first *true simple declarative sentence* I had written.

As a reader, I appreciate the repetition in the Hemingway passage. The effect is like the beat of a bass drum. It vibrates the writer's message into the pores of the skin. Some words — like "true" and "sentence" — act as building blocks and can be repeated to good effect. Distinctive words — like "scrollwork" and "ornament" — deserve their own space.

Observing word territory eliminates repetition, but its best effect is to craft writing with distinctive language in support of the work's purpose. Consider this wonderful rant written by John Kennedy Toole for the lips of Ignatius J. Reilly, the elephantine hero of *A Confederacy of Dunces*. The city in question is New Orleans, and the object of scorn is a police officer who has told Reilly to shove off:

> "This city is famous for its gamblers, prostitutes, exhibitionists, anti-Christs, alcoholics, sodomites, drug addicts, fetishists, onanists, pornographers, frauds, jades, litterbugs . . . all of whom are only too well protected by graft. If you have a moment, I shall endeavor to discuss the crime problem with you, but don't make the mistake of bothering me."

In a paragraph of fifty-three words, only two are repeated ("you" and "the"). The rest is a fountain of interesting language, an inventory of deviance that defined the dark side of the Crescent City before Hurricane Katrina washed so much of it away.

One final piece of advice: Leave *said* alone. Don't be tempted by the muse of variation to permit characters to opine, elaborate, cajole, or chortle.

## WORKSHOP

1. Read something you wrote at least a year ago. Pay attention to the words you repeat. Divide them into three categories: (a) function words (*said, that*), (b) building-block words (*house, river*), and (c) distinctive words (*silhouette, jingle*).

2. Do the same with a new draft. Your goal is to recognize unintended repetition before it is published.

3. Read selections from novels and nonfiction stories that make use of dialogue. Study the attribution, paying close atten-

tion to when the author uses *says* or *said,* and when the writer chooses a more descriptive alternative.

4. Imagine that you have written a draft in which you repeat on a single page of text the following words: *sofa, mouth, house, idea, earthquake, friend.* Consider which of these you might revise with a synonym to avoid repetition.

-◄◦►-

# Play with words, even in serious stories.

*Choose words the average writer avoids
but the average reader understands.*

Just as a sculptor works with clay, a writer shapes a world with words. In fact, the earliest English poets were called *shapers,* artists who molded the stuff of language to create stories the way that God, the Great Shaper, formed heaven and earth.

Good writers play with language, even when the topic is death. "Do not go gentle into that good night," wrote Welsh poet Dylan Thomas to his dying father. "Rage, rage against the dying of the light."

Play and death may seem at odds, but the writer finds ways to connect them. To express his grief, the poet fiddles with language, prefers "gentle" to *gently,* chooses "night" to rhyme with "light," and repeats the word "rage." Later, he will pun about those "grave men, near death, who see with blinding sight." The double meaning of "grave men" leads straight to the oxymoron "blinding sight." Wordplay, even in the shadow of death.

The headline writer is the poet among journalists, stuffing big meaning into small spaces. Consider this headline about a shocking day during the war in Iraq:

**Jubilant mob mauls
4 dead Americans**

The circumstances are hideous: Iraqi civilians attack American security officers, burn them to death in their cars, beat and dismember their charred carcasses, drag them through the street, and hang what's left from a bridge — all while onlookers cheer. Even amid such carnage, the headline writer plays with the language. The writer repeats consonant sounds (*b* and *m*) for emphasis, and contrasts the words "jubilant" and "dead" with surprising effect. "Jubilant" stands out as well chosen, derived from *jubilare*, the Latin verb that means "to raise a shout of joy."

Words like "mob," "dead," and "Americans" appear in news reports all the time. "Mauls" is a verb we might see in a story about a dog attack on a child. But "jubilant" is a distinctive word, comprehensible to most readers, but rare in the context of news.

Too often, writers suppress their vocabularies in a misguided attempt to lower the level of language for a general audience. Obscure words should be defined in texts or made clear from context. But the reading vocabulary of the average citizen is larger than the writing vocabulary of the typical author. As a result, scribes who choose their words from a deeper well attract special attention from readers and gain reputations as "writers."

A rich writing vocabulary does not require big or fancy words. One of America's greatest essayists was M. F. K. Fisher, known for writing about food, but always adding the flavor of playful language to all her work. This vivid childhood memory describes a small room carved out of the side of a garage to house a favorite workman:

> The room had been meant for tools, I assume. It was big enough for a cot, which was always tidy, and an old Morris chair, and a decrepit office desk. The walls were part of the garage, with newspaper darkening on them to keep out the drafts. There was a small round kerosene stove, the kind we sometimes used in our Laguna summer place, with a murky glow through its window and a good warm smell. There was soft light from an overhead bulb. There was a shelf of books, but what they were I never knew. From the roof beams hung slowly twirling bundles of half-cured tobacco

leaves, which Charles got through some strange dealings from Kentucky. He dried them, and every night ground their most brittle leaves into a pipe mixture in the palm of his hand. He would reach up, snap off a leaf, and then sit back in his old chair and talk to us, my sister Anne and the new one Norah and me, until it was time to puff out more delicious fumes. (from *Among Friends*)

Fisher uses no elaborate metaphors here or easy puns. Her play comes in the form of a constellation of precise words and images that transport us from our own time and place to that little room so long ago.

Fisher's restraint stands in sharp contrast to the hallucinatory wordplay in *Act of the Damned* by António Lobo Antunes:

At eight a.m. on the second Wednesday of September, 1975, the alarm clock yanked me up out of my sleep like a derrick on the wharf hauling up a seaweed-smeared car that didn't know how to swim. I surfaced from the sheets, the night dripping from my pajamas and my feet as the iron claws deposited my arthritic cadaver on to the carpet, next to the shoes full of yesterday's smell. I rubbed my fists into my battered eyes and felt flakes of rust fall from the corners. Ana was wrapped, like a corpse in the morgue, in a blanket on the far side of the bed, with only her broomhead of hair poking out. A pathetic shred of leather from a dead heel tumbled off the mattress. I went to the bathroom to brush my teeth and the heartless mirror showed me the damage the years had wrought, as on an abandoned chapel.

Even those who prefer a much plainer style need an occasional swim in a surrealistic sea of language — if only to cleanse us of our word complacency.

All of us possess a reading vocabulary as big as a lake but draw from a writing vocabulary as small as a pond. The good news is that the acts of searching and gathering always expand the number of usable words. The writer sees and hears and records. The seeing leads to language.

"The writer must be able to feel words intimately, one at a time," writes poet Donald Hall in *Writing Well*. "He must also be able to step back, inside his head, and see the flowing sentence. But he starts with the single word." Hall celebrates writers who *"are original, as if seeing a thing for the first time; yet they report their vision in a language that reaches the rest of us*. For the first quality the writer needs imagination; for the second he needs skill. . . . Imagination without skill makes a lively chaos; skill without imagination, a deadly order."

## WORKSHOP

1. Read several stories in today's newspaper. Circle any surprising word, especially one you are not used to seeing in the news.

2. Write a draft with the intention of unleashing your writing vocabulary. Show this draft to test readers and interview them about your word choice and their level of understanding. Share your findings with others.

3. Read the work of a writer you admire, paying special attention to word choice. Circle any signs of playfulness by the writer, especially when the subject matter is serious.

4. Find a writer, perhaps a poet, whose work you read as an inspiration for writing. Circle the words that interest you. Even if you know their meaning, look them up in a historical lexicon, such as the *Oxford English Dictionary*. Find their etymologies. Try to locate their first known use in written English.

# TOOL 14

◄o►

## Get the name of the dog.

*Dig for the concrete and specific,*
*details that appeal to the senses.*

Novelist Joseph Conrad once described his task this way: "by the power of the written word to make you hear, to make you feel — it is, before all, to make you *see.*" When Gene Roberts, a great American newspaper editor, broke in as a cub reporter in North Carolina, he read his stories aloud to a blind editor who would chastise young Roberts for not making him see.

When details of character and setting appeal to the senses, they create an experience for the reader that leads to understanding. When we say "I see," we most often mean "I understand." Inexperienced writers may choose the obvious detail, the man puffing on the cigarette, the young woman chewing on what's left of her fingernails. Those details fail to tell — unless the man is dying of lung cancer or the woman is anorexic.

At the *St. Petersburg Times,* editors and writing coaches warn reporters not to return to the office without "the name of the dog." That reporting task does not require the writer to use the detail in the story, but it reminds the reporter to keep her eyes and ears opened. When Kelley Benham wrote a story about a ferocious rooster that attacked a toddler, she not only got the name of the rooster, Rockadoodle Two, but also the names of his parents, Rockadoodle and one-legged Henny Penny. (I cannot explain why it matters that the offending rooster's mother had only one leg, but it does.)

Before the execution of a serial killer, reporter Christopher Scanlan flew to Utah to visit the family of one of the murderer's presumed victims. Eleven years earlier, a young woman left her house and never returned. Scanlan found the detail that told the story of the family's enduring grief. He noticed a piece of tape over the light switch next to the front door:

> BOUNTIFUL, Utah — Belva Kent always left the front porch light on when her children went out at night. Whoever came home last turned it off, until one day in 1974 when Mrs. Kent told her family: "I'm going to leave that light on until Deb comes home and she can turn it off."

> The Kents' porch light still burns today, night and day. Just inside the front door, a strip of tape covers the switch.

> Deb never came home.

Here's the key: Scanlan *saw* the taped-over switch and asked about it. His curiosity, not his imagination, captured the great detail.

The quest for such details has endured for centuries, as any historical anthology of reportage will reveal. British scholar John Carey describes these examples from his collection *Eyewitness to History:*

> This book is . . . full of unusual or indecorous or incidental images that imprint themselves scaldingly on the mind's eye: the ambassador peering down the front of Queen Elizabeth I's dress and noting the wrinkles; . . . the Tamil looter at the fall of Kuala Lumpur upending a carton of snowy Slazenger tennis balls. . . . Pliny watching people with cushions on their heads against the ash from the volcano; Mary, Queen of Scots, suddenly aged in death, with her pet dog cowering among her skirts and her head

held on by one recalcitrant piece of gristle; the starving Irish with their mouths green from their diet of grass.

(I could find no surviving record of the name of Mary's dog, but learned that it was a Skye terrier, a Scottish breed famous for its loyalty and valor. Then a kind reader, Annette Taylor, messaged me from New Zealand to reveal that the name of the "wee doggie" was Geddon. It was a detail she remembered from helping her daughter with a term paper.)

The good writer uses telling details, not only to inform, but to persuade. In 1963 Gene Patterson wrote a column mourning the murders of four girls in the bombing of a church in Birmingham, Alabama:

> A Negro mother wept in the street Sunday morning in front of a Baptist Church in Birmingham. In her hand she held a shoe, one shoe, from the foot of her dead child. We hold that shoe with her. (from the *Atlanta Constitution*)

Patterson will not permit white southerners to escape responsibility for the murder of those children. He fixes their eyes and ears, forcing them to hear the weeping of the grieving mother, and to see the one small shoe. The writer makes us empathize and mourn and understand. He makes us see.

The details that leave a mark are those that stimulate the senses. Feel how Cormac McCarthy begins the novel *All the Pretty Horses:*

> The candleflame and the image of the candleflame caught in the pierglass twisted and righted when he entered the hall and again when he shut the door. He took off his hat and came slowly forward. The floorboards creaked under his boots. In his black suit he stood in the dark glass where the lilies leaned so palely from their waisted cutglass vase. Along the cold hallway behind him hung the portraits of forebears only dimly known to him all framed in glass and dimly lit above the narrow wainscoting.

He looked down at the guttered candlestub. He pressed his thumbprint in the warm wax pooled on the oak veneer. Lastly he looked at the face so caved and drawn among the folds of funeral cloth, the yellowed moustache, the eyelids paper thin. That was not sleeping. That was not sleeping.

Such prose demands the close attention we'd apply to poetry, starting with that glittering collection of merged nouns ("candleflame," "pierglass," "cutglass," "candlestub," "thumbprint"). More powerful is McCarthy's appeal to the senses. He not only gives us color — black and yellow — for our eyes, but also gifts for our other senses: the smell of burning candles, the sound of creaking floorboards, the feel of wax and oak.

## WORKSHOP

1. Read today's newspaper looking for passages that appeal to the senses. Do the same with a novel.

2. The name of my dog is Rex — and he is the king. Ask a group of colleagues or students to share stories about the names of their pets. Which names reveal the most about the personalities of the owners?

3. With some friends, study the collected work of an outstanding photojournalist. Pretend you are writing a story about the scene captured in a photo. Which details might you select, and in what order would you render them?

4. Most writers appeal to the sense of sight. In your next work, look for opportunities to use details of smell, sound, taste, and touch.

—◄○►—

# Pay attention to names.

*Interesting names attract the writer —*
*and the reader.*

A fondness for interesting names is not a tool, strictly speaking, but a condition, a sweet literary addiction. I once wrote a story about the name Z. Zyzor, the last name listed in the St. Petersburg phone directory. The name turned out to be a fake, made up long ago by postal workers so that family members could call them in an emergency, just by looking up the last name in the phone book. What captured my attention was the name. I wondered what *Z* stood for: Zelda Zyzor? Zorro Zyzor? And what was it like to go through life last in line?

Fiction writers get to make up names for characters, names that become so familiar they become part of our cultural imagination: Rip Van Winkle, Ichabod Crane, Hester Prynne, Captain Ahab, Ishmael, Huckleberry Finn, Jo March, Scarlett O'Hara, Holden Caulfield, Forrest Gump.

Sports and entertainment provide an inexhaustible well of interesting names: Babe Ruth, Jackie Robinson, Mickey Mantle, Johnny Unitas, Zola Budd, Shaquille O'Neal, Venus Williams, Tina Turner, Spike Lee, Marilyn Monroe, Oprah Winfrey, Elvis Presley.

Writers gravitate toward stories that take place in towns with interesting names: Kissimmee, Florida; Bountiful, Utah; Intercourse, Pennsylvania; Moose Jaw, Saskatchewan; Fort Dodge, Iowa; Opp, Alabama.

But the best names seem, as if by magic, attached to real characters who wind up making news. The best reporters recognize and take advantage of coincidence between name and circumstance. A story in the *Baltimore Sun* revealed the sad details of a woman whose devotion to her man led to the deaths of her two young daughters. The mother was Sierra Swann, who, in spite of a lyrical name evoking natural beauty, came apart in a grim environment, "where heroin and cocaine are available curbside beneath the blank stares of boarded-up windows." The writer traced her downfall, not to drugs, but to an "addiction to the companionship of Nathaniel Broadway." Sierra Swann. Nathaniel Broadway. A fiction writer could not invent names more apt and interesting.

I opened my phone book at random and discovered these names on two consecutive pages: Danielle Mall, Charlie Mallette, Hollis Mallicoat, Ilir Mallkazi, Eva Malo, Mary Maloof, John Mamagona, Lakmika Manawadu, Khai Mang, Ludwig Mangold. Names can provide a backstory, suggesting history, ethnicity, generation, and character. (The brilliant and playful American theologian Martin Marty refers to himself as "Marty Marty.")

The writer's interest in names extends beyond person and place to things. Roald Dahl, who would gain fame for writing the novel *Charlie and the Chocolate Factory*, remembers his childhood in sweet shops craving such delights as "Bull's-eyes and Old Fashioned Humbugs and Strawberry Bonbons and Glacier Mints and Acid Drops and Pear Drops and Lemon Drops. . . . My own favourites were Sherbet Suckers and Liquorice Bootlaces." Not to mention the "Gobstoppers" and "Tonsil Ticklers."

For poet Donald Hall, it is not candies but another delicacy of names that captures his imagination in the hilarious ode "O Cheese":

In the pantry the dear dense cheeses, Cheddars and harsh
Lancashires; Gorgonzola with its magnanimous manner;
the clipped speech of Roquefort; and a head of Stilton
that speaks in a sensuous riddling tongue like Druids.

It's hard to think of a writer with more interest in names than Vladimir Nabokov. Perhaps because he wrote in both Russian and English — and had a scientific interest in butterflies — Nabokov dissected words and images, looking for the deeper levels of meaning. His greatest antihero, Humbert Humbert, begins the narration of *Lolita* with this memorable passage:

Lolita, light of my life, fire of my loins. My sin, my soul. Lo-lee-ta:
the tip of the tongue taking a trip of three steps down the palate to
tap, at three, on the teeth. Lo. Lee. Ta.

She was Lo, plain Lo, in the morning, standing four feet ten in
one sock. She was Lola in slacks. She was Dolly at school. She was
Dolores on the dotted line. But in my arms she was always Lolita.

In this great and scandalous novel, Nabokov includes an alphabetical listing of Lolita's classmates, beginning with Grace Angel and concluding with Louise Windmuller. The novel becomes a virtual gazetteer of American place names, from the way we name our motels: "all those Sunset Motels, U-Beam Cottages, Hillcrest Courts, Pine View Courts, Mountain View Courts, Skyline Courts, Park Plaza Courts, Green Acres, Mac's Courts," to the funny names attached to roadside toilets: "Guys-Gals, John-Jane, Jack-Jill and even Buck's-Doe's."

What's in a name? For the attentive writer, and the eager reader, the answer can be fun, insight, charm, aura, character, identity, psychosis, fulfillment, inheritance, decorum, indiscretion, and possession. For in some cultures, if I know your name and can speak it, I own your soul.

## WORKSHOP

1. In the Judeo-Christian story of creation, God grants mankind a special power over other creatures: "When the Lord God formed out of the ground all the beasts of the field and the birds of the air, he brought them to the man to see what he would call them, for that which man called each of them, that would be its name." Have a conversation about the larger religious and cultural implications of naming, including ceremonies of naming such as birth, baptism, conversion, and marriage. Don't forget nicknames, street names, stage names, and pen names. What are the practical implications of naming for writers?

2. J. K. Rowling, the popular author of the Harry Potter series, has a gift for naming. Think of her heroes: Albus Dumbledore, Sirius Black, and Hermione Granger. And her villains: Draco Malfoy and his henchmen Crabbe and Goyle. Read one of the Harry Potter novels, paying special attention to the book's universe of names.

3. In a daybook, keep a record of interesting character and place names you discover in your community.

4. The next time you research a piece of writing, interview an expert who can reveal to you the names of things you do not know: flowers in a garden, parts of an engine, branches of a family tree, breeds of cats. Imagine ways to use such names in your story.

—◄o►—

# Seek original images.

*Reject clichés and first-level creativity.*

The mayor wants to rebuild a dilapidated downtown but will not reveal the details of his plan. You write, "He's playing his cards close to his vest." You have written a cliché, a worn-out metaphor, this one from the world of poker, of course. The mayor's adversaries crave a peek at his hand. Whoever used this metaphor first wrote something fresh, but with overuse it became familiar — and stale.

"Never use a metaphor, simile, or other figure of speech which you are used to seeing in print," writes George Orwell in "Politics and the English Language." Using clichés, he argues, is a substitute for thinking, a form of automatic writing: "Prose consists less and less of *words* chosen for the sake of their meaning, and more and more of *phrases* tacked together like the sections of a prefabricated hen-house." That last phrase is a fresh image, a model of originality.

The language of the people we write about threatens the good writer at every turn. Nowhere is this truer than in the world of sports. A postgame interview with almost any athlete in any sport produces a quilt of clichés:

"We fought hard."
"We stepped up."
"We just tried to have some fun."
"We'll play it one game at a time."

It's a miracle that the best sports writers have always been so original. Consider this description by Red Smith of one of baseball's most famous pitchers:

> This was Easter Sunday, 1937, in Vicksburg, Miss. A thick-muscled kid, rather jowly, with a deep dimple in his chin, slouched out to warm up for the Indians in an exhibition game with the Giants. He had heavy shoulders and big bones and a plowboy's lumbering gait. His name was Bob Feller and everybody had heard about him.

So what is the original writer to do? When tempted by a tired phrase, such as "white as snow," stop writing. Take what the practitioners of natural childbirth call a *cleansing breath*. Then jot down the old phrase on a piece of paper. Start scribbling alternatives:

white as snow
white as Snow White
snowy white
gray as city snow
gray as the London sky
white as the Queen of England

Saul Pett, a reporter known for his style, once told me that he created and rejected more than a dozen images before brainstorming led him to the right one. Such duty to craft should inspire us, but the strain of such effort can be discouraging. Under pressure, write it straight: "The mayor is keeping his plans secret." If you fall back on the cliché, make sure there are no other clichés nearby.

More deadly than clichés of language are what Donald Murray calls "clichés of vision," the narrow frames through which writers learn to see the world. In *Writing to Deadline*, Murray lists common blind spots: victims are always innocent, bureaucrats are lazy, politicians are corrupt, it's lonely at the top, the suburbs are boring.

I have described one cliché of vision as *first-level creativity*. It's impossible, for example, to survive a week of American news without running into the phrase "but the dream became a nightmare." This frame is so pervasive it can be applied to almost any story: the golfer who shoots 33 on the front nine, but 44 on the back; the company CEO jailed for fraud; the woman who suffers from botched plastic surgery. Writers who reach the first level of creativity think they are clever. In fact, they settle for the ordinary, that dramatic or humorous place any writer can reach with minimal effort.

I remember the true story of a Florida man who, walking home for lunch, fell into a ditch occupied by an alligator. The gator bit into the man, who was rescued by firefighters. In a writing workshop, I gave writers a fact sheet from which they wrote five leads for this story in five minutes. Some leads were straight and newsy, others nifty and distinctive, but almost everyone in the room, including me, had this version of a lead sentence: "When Robert Hudson headed home for lunch Thursday, little did he know that he'd become the meal." We agreed that if thirty of us had landed on the same bit of humor, it must be obvious: first-level creativity. We discovered the next level in a lead that read, "Perhaps to a ten-foot alligator, Robert Hudson tastes like chicken." We also agreed that we preferred straight writing to the first pun that came to mind. What value is there in the story of a renegade rooster that falls back on "foul play," or, even worse, "fowl play"?

Fresh language blows a cool breeze through the reader. Think, for example, of all the religious clichés you've encountered about the nature of prayer and compare them to this paragraph by Anne Lamott, from her book *Traveling Mercies:*

Here are the two best prayers I know: "Help me, help me, help me," and "Thank you, thank you, thank you." A woman I know says, for her morning prayer, "Whatever," and then for the evening, "Oh, well," but has conceded that these prayers are more palatable for people without children.

This passage teaches us that originality need not be a burden. A simple shift of context turns the most common and overused expression ("Whatever" or "Oh, well") into a pointed incantation.

## WORKSHOP

1. Read today's newspaper with pencil in hand, and circle any phrase you are used to seeing in print.

2. Do the same with your own work. Circle the clichés and tired phrases. Revise them with straight writing or original images.

3. Brainstorm alternatives to these common similes: red as a rose, white as snow, blue as the sky, cold as ice, hot as hell, hungry as a wolf.

4. Reread some passages from your favorite writer. Can you find any clichés? Circle the most original and vivid images.

—◄○►—

# Riff on the creative language of others.

*Make word lists, free-associate,*
*be surprised by language.*

The day after the vice presidential debate of 2004, I read a clever phrase that contrasted the appearance and styles of the two candidates. Attributed to radio host Don Imus, it described the differences between "Dr. Doom and the Breck Girl." Of course, the dour Dick Cheney was Dr. Doom, and, because of his handsome hair, John Edwards was likened to a pretty girl in a shampoo ad.

By the end of the day, a number of commentators had riffed on this phrase. (*Riff* is a term from jazz used to describe a form of improvisation in which one musician borrows and builds on the musical phrase of another.) The original Imus phrase morphed into "Shrek versus Breck," that is, the ogre versus the hair model.

What followed was a conversation with my witty colleague Scott Libin, who was writing an analysis of the language of political debates. The two of us riffed on the popular distinctions between the two candidates. "Cheney is often described as 'avuncular,'" said Scott. The word means "like an uncle." "Last night he looked more carbuncular than avuncular," I responded, like an angry boil ready to pop.

Like two musicians, Scott and I began to offer variations on our improvisations. Before long, Cheney versus Edwards became:

Dr. No versus Mister Glow
Cold Stare versus Good Hair
Pissed Off versus Well Coiffed

I first suggested Gravitas versus Levitas, gravity versus levity, but Edwards is more toothsome than humorous, so I ventured: Gravitas versus Dental Floss.

Writers collect sharp phrases and colorful metaphors, sometimes for use in their conversation, and sometimes for adaptation into their prose. The danger, of course, is plagiarism, kidnapping the creative work of other writers. No one wants to be known as the Milton Berle of wordsmiths, the stealer of others' best material.

The harmonic way is through the riff. Almost all inventions come out of the associative imagination, the ability to take what is already known and apply it as metaphor to the new. Thomas Edison solved a problem in the flow of electricity by thinking of the flow of water in a Roman aqueduct. Think of how many words have been adapted from old technologies to describe tools of new media: we file, we browse, we surf, we link, we scroll, just to name a few.

The notion that new knowledge derives from old wisdom should liberate the writer from a scrupulous fear of snatching the words of others. The apt phrase then becomes not a temptation to steal — the apple in the Garden of Eden — but a tool to compose your way to the next level of invention.

David Brown riffs on familiar political slogans and ad lingo to offer this devastating critique of America's sheepish inefficiency, especially in times of crisis:

> The sad truth is that despite its success as a sportswear slogan, "Just do it" isn't a terribly popular idea in real American life. We've become a society of rule-followers and permission-seekers. Despite our can-do self image, what we really want is to be told what to do. When the going gets tough, the tough get consent forms.

The writer transforms familiar language into a provocative and contrarian idea: that America is a "can't-do" society.

Let me offer an example from my own work. When I moved from New York to Alabama in 1974, I was struck by the generalized American speech patterns of local broadcast journalists. They did not sound like southerners. In fact, they had been trained to level their regional accents in the interest of comprehensibility. This strategy struck me as more than odd; it seemed like a prejudice against southern speech, an illness, a form of self-loathing.

As I wrote on the topic, I reached a point where I needed to name this language syndrome. I remember sitting on a metal chair at a desk I had constructed out of an old wooden door. What name? What name? It was almost like praying. I thought of the word *disease,* and then remembered the nickname of a college teacher. We called him "The Disease" because his real name was Dr. Jurgalitis. I began to riff: Jurgalitis. Appendicitis. Bronchitis. I almost fell off my chair: Cronkitis!

The essay, now titled "Infectious Cronkitis," was published on the op-ed page of the *New York Times.* I received letters from Walter Cronkite, Dan Rather, and other well-known broadcast journalists who had lived in the South. I was interviewed by Douglas Kiker for *The Today Show.* A couple of years later, I met the editor who had accepted the original column for the *Times.* He told me he liked the essay, but what sold him was the word "Cronkitis":

"A pun in two languages, no less."

"Two languages?" I wondered.

"Yeah, the word *krankheit* in German means 'disease.' Back in vaudeville, the slapstick doctors were called 'Dr. Krankheit.' "

Riffing on language will create wonderful effects you never intended. Which leads me to this additional strategy: always take credit for good writing you did not intend because you'll be getting plenty of criticism for bad writing you did not mean either.

## WORKSHOP

1. In your reading, look for apt phrases, such as the description of plagiarism as "the unoriginal sin." With a friend, riff off these phrases and compare the results. Decide which one you like the best.

2. When you find what seems like a striking, original phrase, conduct a Google search on it. See if you can track its origin or influence.

3. Browse favorite books to find a passage you consider truly original. After reading it a number of times, freewrite in your notebook. Write a parody of what you have read, exaggerating the distinctive elements of style.

—◄○►—

# Set the pace with sentence length.

*Vary sentences to influence the reader's speed.*

I had always found words like *rhythm* and *pace* too subjective, too tonal, to be useful to the writer until I learned how to vary, with a purpose, the lengths of my sentences. Long sentences — I sometimes call them *journey sentences* — create a flow that carries the reader down a stream of understanding, an effect that Don Fry calls "steady advance." A short sentence slams on the brakes.

The writer need not make long sentences elastic, or short ones stubby, to set a tempo for the reader. Consider this passage from *Seabiscuit,* Laura Hillenbrand's book about a famous racehorse:

> As the train lurched into motion, Seabiscuit was suddenly agitated. He began circling around and around the car in distress. Unable to stop him, Smith dug up a copy of *Captain Billy's Whiz Bang* magazine and began reading aloud. Seabiscuit listened. The circling stopped. As Smith read on, the horse sank down into the bedding and slept. Smith drew up a stool and sat by him.

Let me try some word math. The seven sentences in this paragraph average 9.4 words, with this breakdown: 10, 10, 19, 2, 3, 13, 9. The logo-rhythm becomes more interesting when we match sentence length to content. In general, the longer the motion described, the longer the sentence, which is why "Seabiscuit listened" and "The circling stopped" require the fewest words.

The writer controls the pace for the reader, slow or fast or in between, and uses sentences of different lengths to create the music, the rhythm of the story. While these metaphors of sound and speed may seem vague to the aspiring writer, they are grounded in practical questions. How long is the sentence? Where are the period and the comma? How many periods appear in the paragraph?

Writers name three strategic reasons to slow the pace of a story:

1. To simplify the complex
2. To create suspense
3. To focus on the emotional truth

One *St. Petersburg Times* writer strives for comprehensibility in this unusual story about the city government budget:

Do you live in St. Petersburg? Want to help spend $548 million?

It's money you paid in taxes and fees to the government. You elected the City Council to office, and as your representatives, they're ready to listen to your ideas on how to spend it.

Mayor Rick Baker and his staff have figured out how *they'd* like to spend the money. At 7 p.m. Thursday, Baker will ask the City Council to agree with him. And council members will talk about their ideas.

You have the right to speak at the meeting, too. Each resident gets three minutes to tell the mayor and council members what he or she thinks

But why would you stand up?

Because how the city spends its money affects lots of things you care about.

Not every journalist admires this approach to government writing, but its author, Bryan Gilmer, gets credit for achieving what I call *radical clarity*. Gilmer eases the reader into this story with a sequence of short sentences and paragraphs. All the stopping points give the reader time and space to comprehend, yet there is enough variation to imitate the patterns of normal conversation.

Clarity is not the only reason to write short sentences. Let's look at suspense and emotional power, what some call the "Jesus wept" effect. To express Jesus's profound sadness at learning of the death of his friend Lazarus, the Gospel writer uses the shortest possible sentence. Two words. Subject and verb. "Jesus wept."

I learned the power of sentence length when I read a famous essay by Norman Mailer, "The Death of Benny Paret." Mailer has often written about boxing, and here he reports on the night Emile Griffith beat Benny Paret to death in the ring after Paret questioned Griffith's manhood. Mailer's account is riveting, placing us at ringside to witness the terrible event:

> Paret got trapped in a corner. Trying to duck away, his left arm and his head became tangled on the wrong side of the top rope. Griffith was in like a cat ready to rip the life out of a huge boxed rat. He hit him eighteen right hands in a row, an act which took perhaps three or four seconds, Griffith making a pent-up whimpering sound all the while he attacked, the right hand whipping like a piston rod which has broken through the crankcase, or like a baseball bat demolishing a pumpkin.

Notice the rhythm Mailer achieves with three short sentences followed by a long one filled with similes of action and violence. As Paret's fate becomes clearer and clearer, Mailer's sentences get shorter and shorter:

The house doctor jumped into the ring. He knelt. He pried Paret's eyelid open. He looked at the eyeball staring out. He let the lid snap shut. . . . But they saved Paret long enough to take him to a hospital where he lingered for days. He was in a coma. He never came out of it. If he lived, he would have been a vegetable. His brain was smashed.

All that drama. All that raw emotional power. All those short sentences.

In his book *100 Ways to Improve Your Writing,* Gary Provost created this tour de force to demonstrate what happens when the writer experiments with sentences of different lengths:

This sentence has five words. Here are five more words. Five-word sentences are fine. But several together become monotonous. Listen to what is happening. The writing is getting boring. The sound of it drones. It's like a stuck record. The ear demands some variety. Now listen. I vary the sentence length, and I create music. Music. The writing sings. It has a pleasant rhythm, a lilt, a harmony. I use short sentences. And I use sentences of medium length. And sometimes, when I am certain the reader is rested, I will engage him with a sentence of considerable length, a sentence that burns with energy and builds with all the impetus of a crescendo, the roll of the drums, the crash of the cymbals — sounds that say listen to this, it is important.

So write with a combination of short, medium, and long sentences. Create a sound that pleases the reader's ear. Don't just write words. Write music.

## WORKSHOP

1. Review your recent work and examine sentence length. Either by combining sentences or cutting them in half, establish a rhythm that better suits your tone and topic.

2. In reading your favorite authors, become more aware of sentence length. Mark short and long sentences you find effective.

3. Most writers think that a series of short sentences speeds up the reader, but I argue that they slow down the reader, that all those periods are stop signs. Discuss this effect with friends and see if you can reach a consensus.

4. Read some children's books, especially books for very young children, to see if you can gauge the effect on the reader of sentence length variation.

## Tool 19

◄○►

# Vary the lengths of paragraphs.

*Go short or long — or make a turn —*
*to match your intent.*

In a *New York Times* review, critic David Lipsky tears into an author for including in a 207-page book "more than 400 single-sentence paragraphs — a well established distress signal, recognized by book readers and term-paper graders alike." But a distress signal for what? The answer is most likely confusion. The big parts of a story should fit together, but the small parts need some stickum as well. When the big parts fit, we call that good feeling *coherence;* when sentences connect, we call it *cohesion.*

"The paragraph is essentially a unit of thought, not of length," argues British grammarian H. W. Fowler in *Modern English Usage,* the irreplaceable dictionary he compiled in 1926. Such a statement implies that all sentences in a paragraph should be about the same thing and move in a sequence. It also means that writers can break up long paragraphs into parts. They should not, however, paste together paragraphs that are short and disconnected.

Is there, then, an ideal length for a paragraph? In this sequence of paragraphs from the novel *Democracy,* Joan Didion challenges our assumptions about length:

See it this way.

See the sun rise that Wednesday morning in 1975 the way Jack Lovett saw it.

From the operations room at the Honolulu airport.

The warm rain down on the runways.

The smell of jet fuel.

Can five paragraphs in a row be that short? Three of them sentence fragments? Can a sentence fragment be a paragraph?

Again I found answers in *Modern English Usage.* With typical common sense Fowler begins by telling us what the paragraph is for: "The purpose of paragraphing is to give the reader a rest. The writer is saying to him: 'Have you got that? If so, I'll go on to the next point.' " But how much rest does a reader need? Does it depend on subject matter? Genre or medium? The voice of the author? "There can be no general rule about the most suitable length for a paragraph," writes Fowler. "A succession of very short ones is as irritating as very long ones are wearisome."

In a long paragraph, the writer can develop an argument or build a narrative using lots of related examples. In *Ex Libris* by Anne Fadiman, the typical paragraph is more than a hundred words long, with some longer than a full book page. Such length gives Fadiman the space to develop interesting, quirky ideas:

> When I read about food, sometimes a single word is enough to detonate a chain reaction of associative memories. I am like the shoe fetishist who, in order to become aroused, no longer needs to see the object of his desire; merely glimpsing the phrase "spectator pump, size 6½" is sufficient. Whenever I encounter the French word *plein,* which means "full," I am instantly transported back to age fifteen, when, after eating a very large portion of

*poulet à l'estragon,* I told my Parisian hosts that I was *"pleine,"* an adjective that I later learned is reserved for pregnant women and cows in need of milking. The word *ptarmigan* catapults me back ten years to an expedition I accompanied to the Canadian Arctic, during which a polar-bear biologist, tired of canned beans, shot a half dozen ptarmigans. We plucked them, fried them, and gnawed the bones with such ravening carnivorism that I knew on the spot I could never, ever become a vegetarian. Sometimes just the contiguous letters *pt* are enough to call up in me a nostalgic rush of guilt and greed. I may thus be the only person in the world who salivates when she reads the words "ptomaine poisoning."

The writer can use the short paragraph, especially after a long one, to bring the reader to a sudden, dramatic stop. Consider this *New York Times* passage from Jim Dwyer, in which a group of men struggle to escape from a stalled elevator in the World Trade Center, using only a window washer's squeegee as a tool.

They did not know their lives would depend on a simple tool.

After 10 minutes, a live voice delivered a blunt message over the intercom. There had been an explosion. Then the intercom went silent. Smoke seeped into the elevator cabin. One man cursed skyscrapers. Mr. Phoenix, the tallest, a Port Authority engineer, poked for a ceiling hatch. Others pried apart the car doors, propping them open with the long wooden handle of Mr. Demczur's squeegee.

There was no exit.

This technique — a four-word paragraph after one of sixty-four words — can be abused with overuse, but to create surprise it packs a punch.

A solid, unified paragraph can act as a mini-narrative, an anecdote that takes a turn in the middle:

> As soon as I had tightened my bow there was a burst of applause, but I was still nervous. However, as I ran my swollen fingers over the strings, Mozart's phrases came flooding back to me like so many faithful friends. The peasants' faces, so grim a moment before, softened under the influence of Mozart's limpid music like parched earth under a shadow, and then, in the dancing light of the oil lamp, they blurred into one. (from *Balzac and the Little Chinese Seamstress*)

The logic of this paragraph by novelist Dai Sijie is cause and effect, the turn occurring when the sweet music softens the faces of the Chinese peasants.

Another memorable example of a paragraph turn comes from the book *How Soccer Explains the World* by Franklin Foer:

> From the newspaper accounts of the period, it's not at all clear that the Jewish team possessed superior talent. But the clippings do make mention of the enthusiastic Jewish supporters and the grit of the players. The grittiest performance of them all came at the greatest moment in Hakoah history. In the third to last game of the 1924–25 season, an opposing player barreled into Hakoah's Hungarian-born goalkeeper Alexander Fabian as he handled the ball. [Here comes the turn.] Fabian toppled onto his arm, injuring it so badly that he could no longer plausibly continue in goal. This was not an easily remediable problem. The rules of the day precluded substitutions in any circumstance. So Fabian returned to the game with his arm in a sling and swapped positions with a teammate, moving up into attack on the outside right. Seven minutes after the calamitous injury, Hakoah blitzed forward on a counterattack. A player called Erno Schwarz landed the ball at Fabian's feet. With nine minutes remaining in the game, Fabian scored the goal that won the game and clinched Hakoah's championship.

This shapely paragraph helps the writer develop a whole story within a story, complete with exposition, complication, resolution, and payoff at the end.

Too many paragraphs of such length, however, eradicate the white space on a page, and white space is the writer's friend — and the reader's. "Paragraphing is also a matter of the eye," writes Fowler. "A reader will address himself more readily to his task if he sees from the start that he will have breathing-spaces from time to time than if what is before him looks like a marathon course."

## WORKSHOP

1. Read the paragraph above by Anne Fadiman, which contains 203 words. Could you, if necessary, divide it into two or three paragraphs? Discuss your choices with a friend.

2. Check examples of your recent work. Look for strings of long paragraphs and short ones. Can you take some of the long paragraphs and break them into smaller units? Are the one-sentence paragraphs related enough that they can be joined?

3. In your reading of journalism and literature, pay attention to paragraph length. Look for paragraphs that are either very long or very short. Imagine the author's purpose in each case.

4. In your reading, pay attention to the ventilating effects of white space, especially surrounding the ends of paragraphs. Does the writer use that location as a point of emphasis? Do the words at the end of a paragraph shout, "Look at me!"?

5. Read this section again, looking for examples of paragraphs that take a turn in the middle. Look for them in all of your reading.

◄○►

# Choose the number of elements with a purpose in mind.

*One, two, three, or four:*
*each sends a secret message to the reader.*

A self-conscious writer has no choice but to select a specific number of examples or elements in a sentence or paragraph. The writer chooses the number and, when it is greater than one, the order. (If you think the order of a list unimportant, try reciting the names of the four Evangelists in this order: Luke, Mark, John, and Matthew.)

## THE LANGUAGE OF ONE

Let's examine some texts with our X-ray reading glasses, looking beneath the surface meaning to the grammatical machinery at work below.

> That girl is smart.

In this simple sentence, the writer declares a single defining characteristic of the girl: her intelligence. We'll need evidence, to be sure. But, for now, the reader must focus on that particular quality. It is this effect of unity, single-mindedness, no-other-alternativeness, that characterizes the language of one.

Jesus wept.
Call me.
Call me Ishmael.
Go to hell.
Here's Johnny.
I do.
God is love.
Elvis.
Elvis has left the building.
Word.
True.
I have a dream.
I have a headache.
Not now.
Read my lips.

Tom Wolfe once told William F. Buckley Jr. that if a writer wants the reader to think something the absolute truth, the writer should render it in the shortest possible sentence. Trust me.

## THE LANGUAGE OF TWO

We are told "That girl is smart," but what happens when we learn:

That girl is smart and sweet.

The writer has altered our perspective on the world. The choice for the reader is not between smart and sweet. Instead, the writer forces us to hold these two characteristics in our mind at the same time. We have to balance them, weigh them against each other, compare and contrast them.

Mom and dad.
Tom and Jerry.
Ham and eggs.

Abbott and Costello.
Men are from Mars. Women are from Venus.
Dick and Jane.
Rock 'n' roll.
Magic Johnson and Larry Bird.
I and thou.

In *The Ethics of Rhetoric,* Richard M. Weaver explains that the language of two "divides the world."

## THE LANGUAGE OF THREE

With the addition of one, the dividing power of number two turns into what one scholar calls the "encompassing" magic of number three.

That girl is smart, sweet, and determined.

As this sentence grows, we see the girl in a more well-rounded way. Rather than simplify her as smart, or divide her as smart and sweet, we now triangulate the dimensions of her character. In our language and culture, three provides a sense of the whole:

Beginning, middle, and end.
Father, Son, and Holy Ghost.
Moe, Larry, and Curly.
Tinkers to Evers to Chance.
A priest, a minister, and a rabbi.
Executive, legislative, judicial.
The *Niña,* the *Pinta,* and the *Santa Maria.*

At the end of his most famous passage on the nature of love, Saint Paul writes to the Corinthians: "For now, faith, hope, and love abide, these three. But the greatest of all is love." The powerful movement is from trinity to unity, from a sense of the whole to an understanding of what is most important.

## THE LANGUAGE OF FOUR AND MORE

In the anti-math of writing, the number three is greater than four. The mojo of three offers a greater sense of completeness than four or more. Once we add a fourth or fifth detail, we have achieved escape velocity, breaking out of the circle of wholeness:

That girl is smart, sweet, determined, and neurotic.

We can add descriptive elements to infinity. Four or more details in a passage can offer a flowing, literary effect that the best writers have created since Homer listed the names of the Greek tribes. Consider the beginning of Jonathan Lethem's novel *Motherless Brooklyn:*

Context is everything. Dress me up and see. I'm a carnival barker, an auctioneer, a downtown performance artist, a speaker in tongues, a senator drunk on filibuster. *I've got Tourette's.*

If we check these sentences against our theory of numbers, it would reveal this pattern: 1-2-5-1. In the first sentence the author declares a single idea, stated as the absolute truth. In the next sentence, he gives the reader two imperative verbs. In the next, he spins five metaphors. In the final sentence, the writer returns to a definitive declaration — so important he casts it in italics.

So good writing is as easy as one, two, three — and four.

In summary:

- Use one for power.
- Use two for comparison, contrast.
- Use three for completeness, wholeness, roundness.
- Use four or more to list, inventory, compile, and expand.

### WORKSHOP

1. In your reading, notice passages where the writer uses the number of examples to achieve a specific effect.

2. Reread examples of your recent work. Examine your use of numbers. Look for cases in which you might add an example or subtract one to create the effects described above.

3. Brainstorm with friends to list examples of the use of one, two, three, and four. Draw these from proverbs, everyday speech, music lyrics, famous orations, literature, and sports.

4. Look for an opportunity to use a long list in your writing. (For example, the names of kittens in a litter. The items in the window of an old drugstore. Objects abandoned at the bottom of a swimming pool.) Play with the order to achieve the best effect.

# TOOL 21

—◄◦►—

## Know when to back off and when to show off.

*When the topic is most serious, understate;*
*when least serious, exaggerate.*

In "Why I Write," George Orwell explains that "good prose is like a window pane." The best work calls the reader's attention to the world being described, not to the writer's flourishes. When we peer out a window onto the horizon, we don't notice the pane, yet the pane frames our vision just as the writer frames our view of the story.

Most writers have at least two modes. One says, "Pay no attention to the writer behind the curtain. Look only at the world." The other says, without inhibition, "Watch me dance. Aren't I a clever fellow?" In rhetoric, these two modes have names. The first is called *understatement*. The second is called *overstatement* or *hyperbole*.

Here's a tool of thumb that works for me: The more serious or dramatic the subject, the more the writer backs off, creating the effect that the story tells itself. The more playful or inconsequential the topic, the more the writer can show off. Back off or show off.

Consider John Hersey's opening to *Hiroshima:*

At exactly fifteen minutes past eight in the morning, on August 6, 1945, Japanese time, at the moment when the atomic bomb flashed above Hiroshima, Miss Toshiko Sasaki, a clerk in the personnel department of the East Asia Tin Works, had just sat down at her place in the plant office and was turning her head to speak to the girl in the next desk.

Described by some as the most important work of nonfiction in the twentieth century, this book begins with the most ordinary of circumstances, a recitation of the time and date, with two office workers about to converse. The flash of the atomic bomb hides inside that sentence. Because we imagine the horror to follow, Hersey's understatement creates the anxiety of anticipation.

Here is how Mikal Gilmore, the brother of infamous killer Gary Gilmore, begins *Shot in the Heart:*

> I have a story to tell. It is a story of murder told from inside the house where murder is born. It is the house where I grew up, a house that, in some ways, I have never been able to leave. And if I ever hope to leave this place, I must tell what I know. So let me begin.

The events of this story are brutal and tragic, yet Gilmore's monosyllabic prose is as spare as a cell on death row.

Contrast such understatement to the razzmatazz of Saul Pett, who wrote this description of New York City's sprightly mayor Ed Koch for the Associated Press:

> He is the freshest thing to blossom in New York since chopped liver, a mixed metaphor of a politician, the antithesis of the packaged leader, irrepressible, candid, impolitic, spontaneous, funny, feisty, independent, uncowed by voter blocs, unsexy, unhandsome, unfashionable and altogether charismatic, a man oddly at peace with himself in an unpeaceful place, a mayor who presides over the country's largest Babel with unseemly joy.

Pett's prose is vaudevillian, over-the-top, a little song, a little dance, a squirt of seltzer down your pants — as was Mayor Koch. Although municipal politics can be serious business, the context here allows Pett space for a full theatrical review.

The clever überwriter can, in the words of Anna Quindlen, "write your way onto page one," as investigative reporter Bill Nottingham did the day his city editor assigned him to cover the local spelling bee for the *St. Petersburg Times:* "Thirteen-year-old Lane Boy is to spelling what Billy the Kid was to gun-fighting, icy-nerved and unflinchingly accurate."

To understand the difference between understatement and overstatement, consider the cinematic difference between two Steven Spielberg movies. In *Schindler's List,* Spielberg evokes the catastrophes of the Holocaust rather than depict them in graphic detail. In a black-and-white movie, he makes us follow the trials and inevitable death of one little Jewish girl dressed in red. *Saving Private Ryan* reveals the gruesome effects of warfare on the shores of France during the invasion of Normandy, complete with severed limbs and spurting arteries, all in color. I, for one, favor the more restrained approach, where the artist leaves room for my imagination.

"If it sounds like writing," writes hard-boiled novelist Elmore Leonard, "I rewrite it."

## WORKSHOP

1. Keep your eyes open for lively stories that make their way onto page one of the newspaper, even though they lack traditional news value. Discuss how they were written and what might have appealed to the editor.

2. Review some of the stories written after great tragedies, such as the destruction of New Orleans by Hurricane Katrina, or the 2004 tsunami that killed thousands in Southeast Asia. Notice the difference between the stories that feel restrained and the ones that seem overwritten.

3. Read some examples of feature obituaries from the book produced by the *New York Times,* titled *Portraits of Grief.* Study the understated ways in which these are written.

4. Read works of humor from writers such as Woody Allen, Roy Blount Jr., Dave Barry, S. J. Perelman, and Steve Martin. Look for examples of both hyperbole and understatement.

# Climb up and down the ladder of abstraction.

*Learn when to show, when to tell,*
*and when to do both.*

Good writers move up and down a ladder of language. At the bottom are bloody knives and rosary beads, wedding rings and baseball cards. At the top are words that reach for a higher meaning, words like *freedom* and *literacy*. Beware of the middle, the rungs of the ladder where bureaucracy and technocracy lurk. Halfway up, teachers are referred to as *full-time equivalents,* and school lessons are called *instructional units.*

The ladder of abstraction remains one of the most useful models of thinking and writing ever invented. Popularized by S. I. Hayakawa in his 1939 book *Language in Action,* the ladder has been adopted and adapted in hundreds of ways to help people ponder language and express meaning.

The easiest way to make sense of this tool is to begin with its name: *the ladder of abstraction.* That name contains two nouns. The first is *ladder,* a specific tool you can see, hold with your hands, and climb. It involves the senses. You can do things with it. Put it against a tree to rescue your cat Voodoo. The bottom of the ladder rests on concrete language. Concrete is hard, which is why when you fall off the ladder from a high place, you might break your foot. Your right foot. The one with the spider tattoo.

The second noun is *abstraction.* You can't eat it or smell it or measure it. It is not easy to use as a case study. It appeals not to the senses, but to the intellect. It is an idea that cries out for exemplification.

A 1964 essay by John Updike begins, "We live in an era of gratuitous inventions and negative improvements." That language is general and abstract, near the top of the ladder. It provokes our thinking, but what concrete evidence leads Updike to his conclusion? The answer is in his second sentence: "Consider the beer can." To be even more specific, Updike complained that the invention of the pop-top ruined the aesthetic experience of opening a can of beer. *Pop-top* and *beer* rest at the bottom of the ladder, *aesthetic experience* at the top.

We learned this language lesson in kindergarten when we played show-and-tell. When we showed the class our 1957 Mickey Mantle baseball card, we were at the bottom of the ladder. When we told the class about what a great season Mickey had in 1956, we started to climb the ladder, toward the meaning of *greatness*.

Here's Updike again in his novel *Marry Me:*

> Outside their bedroom windows, beside the road, stood a giant elm, one of the few surviving in Greenwood. New leaves were curled in the moment after the bud unfolds, their color sallow, a dusting, a veil not yet dense enough to conceal the anatomy of branches. The branches were sinuous, stately, constant: an inexhaustible comfort to her eyes. Of all things accessible to Ruth's vision the elm most nearly persuaded her of a cosmic benevolence. If asked to picture God, she would have pictured this tree.

Just as he moved down the ladder from "gratuitous inventions" to "beer can," here Updike goes the other way, gaining the altitude of meaning by climbing this "giant elm" toward "cosmic benevolence."

Carolyn Matalene, an influential writing teacher from South Carolina, taught me that when I write prose that the reader can neither see nor understand, I'm probably trapped halfway up the ladder. What does language look like from that halfway vantage point? Let me answer with a story about one of my favorite schools in Florida, Marjorie Kinnan Rawlings Elementary. Since 1992 the teachers have dedicated themselves to helping every child learn to write. During a workshop there, I asked the principal if the school had developed a mission statement. She sent a helper to fetch a fancy, laminated page:

> Our mission is to improve student achievement and thereby prepare students for continued learning in middle school and high school. This learning community will accomplish this mission by developing and implementing world class learning systems. Alignment will be monitored by continual application of quality principles and responsiveness to customer expectations.

I'm not making this up. I've got the original in my office if you'd like to see it. How did it wind up in my office? In an act of vigilante dedication to good writing, I stole it. Before long, the principal sent me a little card with the new mission statement, this one free of jargon and numbing bureaucratic language. It reads: "Our mission: Learning to write, writing to learn." Because I love the teachers and the principal, I proclaim this the greatest revision of the twentieth century.

One of America's finest baseball writers, Thomas Boswell, wrote in an essay on the aging of athletes:

> The cleanup crews come at midnight, creeping into the ghostly quarter-light of empty ballparks with their slow-sweeping brooms and languorous, sluicing hoses. All season, they remove the inanimate refuse of a game. Now, in the dwindling days of September and October, they come to collect baseball souls.
>
> Age is the sweeper, injury his broom.
>
> Mixed among the burst beer cups and the mustard-smeared wrappers headed for the trash heap, we find old friends who are

being consigned to the dust bin of baseball's history. (from the
*Washington Post*)

The abstract "inanimate refuse" soon becomes visible as "burst
beer cups" and "mustard-smeared wrappers." And those cleanup
crews with their very real brooms and hoses transmogrify into
grim reapers in search of "baseball souls."

Metaphors and similes help us understand abstractions
through comparison with concrete things. "Civilization is a
stream with banks," wrote Will Durant in *LIFE* magazine, working both ends of the ladder. "The stream is sometimes filled with
blood from people killing, stealing, shouting and doing the
things historians usually record, while on the banks, unnoticed,
people build homes, make love, raise children, sing songs, write
poetry and even whittle statues. The story of civilization is the
story of what happened on the banks. Historians are pessimists
because they ignore the banks for the river."

Two questions will help you make this tool work. "Can you
give me an example?" will drive the speaker down the ladder. But
"What does that mean?" will carry him aloft.

## WORKSHOP

1. Read with the distinction between abstract and concrete
in your head. Be alert to moments when you need an example, or
when you want to reach for a higher meaning. Notice if the level
of language moves from the concrete to the more abstract.

2. Find essays and reports about bureaucracy and public policy that seem stuck in the middle of the ladder of abstraction.
What kind of reporting or research would be necessary to climb
down or up, to help the reader see or understand?

3. Listen to song lyrics to hear how the language moves on
the ladder of abstraction. "Freedom's just another word for
nothin' left to lose." Or "War, what is it good for, absolutely
nothin'." Or "Give me a sista, I can't resist her, red beans and rice

didn't miss her." Notice how concrete words and images in music express abstractions such as love, hope, lust, and fear.

4. Read several of your stories and describe, in three words or less, what each story is *really* about. Is it about friendship, loss, legacy, betrayal? Are there ways to make such higher meanings clearer to the reader by being even more specific?

# TOOL 23

—◦—

# Tune your voice.

*Read stories aloud.*

Of all effects created by writers, none is more important or elusive than that quality called *voice*. Good writers, it is said time and again, want to find their voice. And they want that voice to be *authentic*, a word that reminds me of *author* and *authority*.

But what is voice, and how does the writer tune it?

The most useful definition comes from my friend and colleague Don Fry: "Voice is the sum of all the strategies used by the author to create the illusion that the writer is speaking directly to the reader from the page." The most important words in that definition are "create," "illusion," and "speaking": voice is an effect created by the writer that reaches the reader through his ears, even when he is receiving the message through his eyes.

Poet David McCord remembers that he once picked up an old copy of *St. Nicholas* magazine, which printed stories written by children. One story caught his attention, and he was "suddenly struck by a prose passage more earthy and natural in voice than what I had been glancing through. This sounds like E. B. White, I said to myself. Then I looked at the signature: Elwyn Brooks White, age 11." McCord recognized the elements of style — the voice — of the young author who would one day grow up to write *Charlotte's Web*.

If Fry is correct, that voice is the "sum" of all writing strategies, which of those strategies are essential to creating the illusion of speech? To answer that question, think of a piece of sound equipment called a graphic equalizer. This is the device that creates the range of sounds in an amplifier by providing about thirty dials or levers, controlling such things as bass and treble. Push up the bass, pull down the treble, add a little reverb to configure the desired sound.

So, if we all had a handy-dandy writing-voice modulator, what ranges would the levers control? Here are a few, expressed as a set of questions:

- *What is the level of language?* That is to say, does the writer use street slang or the logical argument of a professor of metaphysics? Is the level of language at the bottom of the ladder of abstraction or near the top? Does it move up and down?
- *What "person" does the writer work in?* Does the writer use *I* or *we* or *you* or *they* or all of these?
- *What are the range and the source of allusions?* Do these come from high or low culture, or both? Does the writer cite a medieval theologian or a professional wrestler? Or both?
- *How often does the writer use metaphors and other figures of speech?* Does the writer want to sound more like the poet, whose work is rich with figurative images, or the journalist, who uses them for special effect?
- *What is the length and structure of the typical sentence?* Are sentences short and simple? Long and complex? Or mixed?
- *What is the distance from neutrality?* Is the writer trying to be objective, partisan, or passionate?
- *How does the writer frame her material?* Is she on beat or offbeat? Does the writer work with standard subject matter, using conventional story forms? Or is she experimental and iconoclastic?

Consider this passage, a CBS radio broadcast by Edward R. Murrow, on the liberation of the Buchenwald concentration camp in 1945. Read it aloud to experience the voice of the writer:

> We entered. It was floored with concrete. There were two rows of bodies stacked up like cordwood. They were thin and very white. Some of the bodies were terribly bruised, though there seemed to be little flesh to bruise. Some had been shot through the head, but they bled but little. All except two were naked. I tried to count them as best I could and arrived at the conclusion that all that was mortal of more than five hundred men and boys lay there in two neat piles.

The journalist grounds his report in the language of eyewitness testimony. I can hear the struggle between the professional reporter and the outraged human being. The level of language is concrete and vivid, describing terrible things to see. He uses a single chilling simile, "stacked up like cordwood," but the rest seems plain and straightforward. The sentences are mostly short and simple. His writing voice is not neutral — how could it be? — but it describes the world he sees and not the emotions of the reporter. Yet he places himself on the scene in the last sentence, using "I" to give no doubt that he has seen this with his own eyes. The phrase "all that was mortal" sounds literary, as if it had come from Shakespeare. This brief X-ray reading of Murrow's work shows the interaction of the various strategies that create the effect we know as voice.

How different is the effect when seventeenth-century English philosopher Thomas Hobbes describes the passions of mankind:

> Grief for the calamity of another is PITY, and arises from the imagination that the like calamity may befall himself, and therefore is called also COMPASSION, and in the phrase of this present time a FELLOW-FEELING. (from *Leviathan*)

The Murrow passage, with its particularity, evokes pity and compassion. The Hobbes passage, with its abstractions, defines them.

If you write like Murrow, you will sound like a journalist. If you write like Hobbes, you will sound like a philosopher.

The bible for parents of baby boomers was *Baby and Child Care* by Dr. Benjamin Spock, first published in 1945. In the foreword he writes:

> The most important thing I have to say is that you should not take too literally what is said in this book. Every child is different, every parent is different, every illness or behavior problem is somewhat different from every other. All I can do is describe the most common developments and problems in the most general terms. Remember that you are more familiar with your child's temperament and patterns than I could ever be.

Dr. Spock's language is plain but authoritative, his voice wise but modest. He addresses the reader directly, as in a letter, using both "you" and "I," and honors the parent's experience and expertise. No wonder generations of families turned to this voice of the family doctor for advice and peace of mind.

To test your writing voice, the most powerful tool on your workbench is oral reading. Read your story aloud to hear if it sounds like you. When teachers offer this advice to writers, we often meet skeptical glances. "You can't be serious," say these looks. "You don't *literally* mean that I should read the story aloud? Perhaps you mean I should read the story 'in loud,' quietly, with my lips moving?"

No, I mean out loud, and loud enough so that others can hear.

The writer can read the story aloud to herself or to an editor. The editor can read the story aloud to the writer, or to another editor. It can be read this way to receive its voice, or to modulate it. It can be read in celebration, but should never be read in derision. It can be read to hear the problems that must be solved.

Writers complain about tone-deaf editors who read with their eyes and not with their ears. The editor may see an unnecessary phrase, but what does its deletion do to the rhythm of the sentence? That question is best answered by oral — and aural — reading.

## WORKSHOP

1. Read your writing aloud to a friend. Ask, "Does this sound like me?" Discuss the response.

2. After rereading your work, make a list of adjectives that define your voice, such as *heavy* or *aggressive, ludicrous* or *tentative.* Now try to identify the evidence in your writing that led you to these conclusions.

3. Read a draft of a story aloud. Can you hear problems in the story that you could not see?

4. Save the work of writers whose voices appeal to you. Consider why you admire the voice of a particular writer. How is it like your voice? How is it different? In a piece of freewriting, imitate that voice.

PART THREE

# Blueprints

# TOOL 24

◄o►

# Work from a plan.

*Index the big parts of your work.*

Good work has parts: beginning, middle, and ending. Even writers who achieve a seamless tapestry can point out the invisible stitching. A writer who knows the big parts can name them for the reader, using such markers as subheadings and chapter titles. The reader who sees the big parts is more likely to remember the whole story.

The best way to illustrate this effect is to reveal the big parts of a short and deceptively simple children's song, "Three Blind Mice." Sing the melody in your head. Now try to name the parts. Part one is a simple musical phrase repeated once:

> Three blind mice, three blind mice,

Part two builds on that phrase and adds a beat:

> See how they run, see how they run!

Part three adds three equal but more complex phrases:

> They all ran after the farmer's wife,
> Who cut off their tails with a carving knife,
> Did you ever see such a thing in your life

Part four repeats the first phrase, "three blind mice," closing the song into a tight circle:

As three blind mice?

We remember songs because of their transparent structure: verse, verse, chorus, bridge, verse, chorus, instrumental, verse, chorus. The delightful sounds of songs may veil the mechanics of structure, but the architecture of music becomes perceptible with more careful listening and knowing how to name the parts.

Which leads me to the dreaded *O* word, the hellmouth of young writers.

Many writers of the old school were required to hand in outlines with drafts of our stories. Such outlines looked something like this:

    I.
       A.
       B.
          1.
          2.
             a.
             b.
       C.
    II.

And so on.

Here was my problem: I could never see far enough ahead to plot what the third part of section C was going to be. I had to write my way to that point; I had to discover what I was going to say. And so, as a survival mechanism, I invented the reverse outline. I would write a full draft of the story and then create the outline. This turned out to be a useful tool: if I could not write the outline from the story, it meant that I could not discern the parts from the whole, revealing problems of organization.

Although I still don't work from a formal outline, I write a plan, usually a few phrases scribbled on a yellow pad. And here's another tool I learned: an informal plan is nothing more than the Roman numerals required by a formal outline. In other words, my plan helps me see the big parts of the story.

Here's a plan for an obituary of entertainer Ray Bolger, the beloved scarecrow of *The Wizard of Oz:*

    I. Lead with image and dialogue from *Oz.*
   II. Great moments in his dance career other than *Oz.*
  III. His signature song: "Once in Love with Amy."
  IV. His youth: how he became a dancer.
   V. His television career.
  VI. A final image from *Oz.*

I constructed this reverse outline from a close reading of Tom Shales's award-winning work in the *Washington Post.*

When the story grows to any significant length, the writer should label the parts. If the story evolves into a book, the chapters will have titles. In a newspaper or magazine, the parts may carry subheadlines or subtitles. Writers should write these subtitles themselves — *even if the publisher does not use them.*

Here's why: Subtitles will make visible to the busy copyeditor and time-starved reader the big parts of the story. The act of writing them will test the writer's ability to identify and label those parts. And, when well written, these subheads will reveal at a glance the global structure of the piece, indexing the parts, and creating additional points of entry.

In 1994, the courageous American editor Gene Patterson wrote an article for the *St. Petersburg Times* titled "Forged in Battle: The Formative Experience of War." The occasion was the fiftieth anniversary of the invasion of Normandy. Patterson fought in World War II as a young tank platoon leader in Patton's army. His mini-epic begins in medias res, in the middle of things:

> I did not want to kill the two German officers when we met by mistake in the middle of the main street of Gera Bronn.

They somersaulted from their motorcycle when it rounded a corner directly ahead of my column of light armor. They scrambled
to their feet, facing me 20 yards in front of the cannon and machine gun muzzles of my lead armored car, and stood momentar-
ily still as deer. The front wheel of their flattened motorcycle spun
on in the silence.

This passage introduces a meaty memoir of war. Five strong subheadlines index the body of the work:

A Man of the 20th Century
Lead with the Heaviest Punch
From the Georgia Soil
Senseless Dying
Two Certainties about War

Notice how the reader can predict the structure and content of
Patterson's essay from these subtitles alone. They divide the story
into its big parts, name them, and make visible a movement of
theme, logic, and chronology that readers can perceive and remember.

## WORKSHOP

1. Shakespeare's plays are divided into five acts, each divided
into scenes. Read a comedy and a tragedy, such as *As You Like It*
and *Macbeth,* paying attention to the structure of the play and
what Shakespeare tries to accomplish in each of the big parts.

2. Find the longest piece you have written in the last year.
Using a pencil, mark it up according to its parts. Now label those
parts with headings and subheadings.

3. Over the next month, pay attention to the structure of the
fiction you read. Notice the point where you begin to perceive the
global structure of the work. After you finish the work, go back
and review the chapter titles and their effect on your expectations as a reader.

4. Listening to music helps writers learn the structures of composition. As you listen, see if you can recognize the big parts of songs.

5. For your next story, try working from an informal plan that plots the three to six big parts of the work. Revise the plan if necessary.

—◄○►—

# Learn the difference between reports and stories.

*Use one to render information,*
*the other to render experience.*

Journalists use the word *story* with romantic promiscuity. They think of themselves as the wandering minstrels of the modern world, the tellers of tales, the spinners of yarns. And then, too often, they write dull reports.

Reports need not be dull, nor stories interesting. But the difference between *story* and *report* is crucial to the reader's expectation and the writer's execution. Bits of story — call them *anecdotes* — appear in many reports. But the word *story* has a special meaning, and stories have specific requirements that create predictable effects.

What are the differences between *report* and *story,* and how can the writer use them to strategic advantage?

A wonderful scholar named Louise Rosenblatt argued that readers read for two reasons: information and experience. There's the difference. Reports convey information. Stories create experience. Reports transfer knowledge. Stories transport the reader, crossing boundaries of time, space, and imagination. The report points us there. The story puts us there.

A report sounds like this: The school board will meet Thursday to discuss the new desegregation plan.

A story sounds like this: Wanda Mitchell shook her fist at the school board chairman, tears streaming down her face.

The tool sets to create reports and stories also differ. The famous "Five *W*s and *H*" have helped writers gather and convey information with the reader's interests in mind. *Who, what, where,* and *when* appear as the most common elements of information. The *why* and the *how* are harder to achieve. Used in reports, these pieces of information are frozen in time, fixed so readers can scan and understand.

Watch what happens when we unfreeze them, when information is transformed into narrative. In this process of conversion:

*Who* becomes *Character.*
*What* becomes *Action.* (What happened.)
*Where* becomes *Setting.*
*When* becomes *Chronology.*
*Why* becomes *Cause* or *Motive.*
*How* becomes *Process.* (How it happened.)

The writer must figure out whether a project requires the crafting of a report, a story, or some combination of the two. Author and teacher Jon Franklin argues that stories require rising and falling actions, complications, points of insight, and resolutions. While novelists invent these movements in a story, nonfiction writers must report them. In the 1960s Tom Wolfe demonstrated how to match truthful reporting with fictional techniques, such as setting scenes, finding details of character, capturing dialogue, and shifting points of view.

Narrative requires a story and a storyteller. In this scene from *Reading Lolita in Tehran,* Azar Nafisi narrates a surprising moment in one of her secret literature classes:

> I ask, Who can dance Persian-style? Everyone looks at Sanaz. She is shy and refuses to dance. We start to tease her and goad her on, and form a circle around her. As she begins to move, self-

consciously at first, we start to clap and murmur a song. Nassrin cautions us to be quieter. Sanaz begins shyly, taking graceful little steps, moving her waist with a lusty grace. As we laugh and joke more, she becomes bolder; she starts to move her head from side to side, and every part of her body asserts itself, vying for attention with the other parts. Her body quivers as she takes her small steps and dances with her fingers and her hands. A special look has appeared on her face. It is daring and beckoning, designed to attract, to pull in, but at the same time it retracts and refracts with a power she loses as soon as she stops dancing.

This passage moves me every time I read it. I may be a stranger to the author's gender, religion, culture, country, and political system, yet for the seconds it takes to read these words I am transported. She puts me in that room, where I stand in that circle of Iranian women, seduced by the dancer's charms.

South African writer Henk Rossouw combines story and report to good effect. With a single sentence he moves us to another time and place, and to a desperate experience:

When Akallo Grace Grall woke up, she could feel the cool night air on her face, but she couldn't move. Most of her body was under sand. Where was her gun? If she'd lost it, her commander in the Lord's Resistance Army would beat her up. As she dragged herself out of the shallow grave, everything that had happened that day came back to her.

To learn why the life of this African woman deserves special attention, Rossouw explains how she made the journey from "hell to college." To help us grasp the rigor of that journey, Rossouw turns from story to report mode:

In sub-Saharan Africa, only one-quarter of the students enrolled in postsecondary education are women, according to a World Bank estimate from the mid-1990s. About 60 percent of African women live a life that consists of working the land and raising children. Ugandan women bear an average of 6.8 children, and early marriages are encouraged, with rural women marrying as young as 14 years of age. Uganda awards 900 scholarships each year to help women get into college: 10,000 women apply for them. (from the *Chronicle of Higher Education*)

By combining story and report, the writer can speak to both our hearts and our heads, creating sympathy and understanding.

## WORKSHOP

1. Look at the newspaper with the distinction between reports and stories in mind. Look for narrative opportunities missed. Look for bits of stories embedded in reports.

2. Take the same approach to your own work. Look for stories, or at least passages in stories, where you transport the reader to the scene. Search for places in your reports where you might have included story elements.

3. Reread the conversion list for the Five Ws and H. Keep it handy the next time you research and write. Use it to transform report elements into the building blocks of a story.

4. The next time you read a novel, look for the ways in which the author weaves information about politics or history or geography into the tapestry of narrative. How can you apply these techniques in your own work?

—◄◦►—

# Use dialogue as a form of action.

*Dialogue advances narrative; quotes delay it.*

Novelist Elmore Leonard advised writers "to leave out the part that readers tend to skip" and to focus on what they read. But which part is that? He condemns:

> Thick paragraphs of prose you can see have too many words in them. What the writer is doing, he's writing, perpetrating hoopte-doodle, perhaps taking another shot at the weather, or has gone into the character's head, and the reader either knows what the guy's thinking or doesn't care. I'll bet you don't skip dialogue. (from the *New York Times*)

Leonard must have my reading habits in mind, the thousand times I've looked down a gray pillar of text to find the airy white space that ventilates dialogue. Human speech, captured as dialogue on the page, attracts the eyes of the reader and, if done well, advances the story.

Consider this scene from Michael Chabon's novel *The Amazing Adventures of Kavalier & Clay:*

> She turned now and looked at her nephew. "You want to draw comic books?" she asked him.

Joe stood there, head down, a shoulder against the door frame. While Sammy and Ethel argued, he had been affecting to study in polite embarrassment the low-pile, mustard-brown carpeting, but now he looked up, and it was Sammy's turn to feel embarrassed. His cousin looked him up and down, with an expression that was both appraising and admonitory.

"Yes, Aunt," he said. "I do. Only I have one question. What is a comic book?"

Sammy reached into his portfolio, pulled out a creased, well-thumbed copy of the latest issue of *Action Comics*, and handed it to his cousin.

In many ways dialogue defines a story because its power drags us to the scene and sets our ears to the action.

Reporters capture human speech with a purpose different from novelists. They use speech on the page not as action but as an action stopper, a place in the text where characters comment on what has happened. This technique has different names in different media. In print an effective bit of human speech is called a *quote*. Television reporters tag it a *sound bite*. Radio folks struggle under the awkward word *actuality* — because someone actually said it.

The *St. Paul Pioneer Press* covered the sad story of Cynthia Schott, a thirty-one-year-old television anchor who wasted away and died from an eating disorder.

"I was there. I know how it happened," says Kathy Bissen, a friend of Schott's from the TV station. "Everybody did what they individually thought was best. And together, we covered the spectrum of possibilities of how to interact with someone you know has an illness. And yet, none of it made a difference. And you just think to yourself, 'How can this happen?' "

The writer follows advice often given to new reporters: get a good quote high in the story. A good quote offers these benefits:

- It introduces a human voice.
- It explains something important about the subject.
- It frames a problem or dilemma.
- It adds information.
- It reveals the character or personality of the speaker.
- It introduces what is next to come.

But quotes also contain a serious weakness. Consider this quote from a page one story in the *New York Times:* "Less than two percentage points we can handle just by not eating out as much." This quote comes from a woman named Joyce Diffenderfer on how her family copes with mounting credit card debt. But where is Joyce Diffenderfer when she speaks these words? In her kitchen? At the desk where she pays her bills? In her workplace? Most quotes — as opposed to dialogue — are dis-placed. The words are spoken above or outside the action. Quotes are about the action, not in the action. That's why quotes interrupt the progress of the narrative.

Which returns us to the power of dialogue. While quotes provide information or explanation, dialogue thickens the plot. The quote may be heard, but dialogue is overheard. The writer who uses dialogue transports us to a place and time where we get to experience the events described in the story.

Journalists use dialogue infrequently, so the effect stands out like a palm tree in a meadow. Consider this passage by Pulitzer Prize–winning reporter Thomas French on the trial of a Florida firefighter accused of a horrible crime against his neighbor:

> His lawyer called out his name. He stood up, put his hand on a Bible and swore to tell the truth and nothing but. He sat down in the witness box and looked toward the jurors so they could see his face and study it and decide for themselves what kind of man he was.

> "Did you rape Karen Gregory?" asked his lawyer.

"No sir, I did not."

"Did you murder Karen Gregory?"

"No sir." (from the *St. Petersburg Times*)

The inhibitions against dialogue in nonfiction are unfounded. Although dialogue can be recovered and reconstructed from careful research, using multiple sources and appropriate attribution, it can also be overheard. An angry exchange between the mayor and a city council member can be recorded and published. The writer who did not witness testimony from a trial can recover accurate dialogue from court transcripts, often available as public records.

The skillful writer can use both dialogue and quotes to create different effects in the same story, as in this example from the *Philadelphia Inquirer:*

"It looked like two planes were fighting, Mom," Mark Kessler, 6, of Wynnewood, told his mother, Gail, after she raced to the school.

The boy had just witnessed the midair collision of a plane and a helicopter, an accident that dropped deadly wreckage atop an elementary school playground. We've already seen another passage from the same story:

"It was one horrible thing to watch," said Helen Amadio, who was walking near her Hampden Avenue home when the crash occurred. "It exploded like a bomb. Black smoke just poured."

Helen Amadio offers us a true quote, spoken directly to the reporter. Notice the difference between that quote and the implied dialogue between the young boy and his mother. The six-year-old describes the scene to his frantic mom. In other words, the dialogue puts us on the scene where we can overhear the characters in action.

On rare occasions, the reporter combines the information of the quote and the emotional power of dialogue, but only when the source speaks in the immediate aftermath of the event, and only when the reporter focuses on both words and actions. Rick Bragg carries this off in his story on the Oklahoma City bombing:

> "I just took part in a surgery where a little boy had part of his brain hanging out of his head," said Terry Jones, a medical technician, as he searched in his pocket for a cigarette. Behind him, firefighters picked carefully through the skeleton of the building, still searching for the living and the dead.
>
> "You tell me," he said, "how can anyone have so little respect for human life." (from the *New York Times*)

Leave out the parts readers tend to skip; make room for the parts they can't resist.

## WORKSHOP

1. Read the newspaper for quotes and fiction for dialogue. Think about their different effects on the reader.

2. Look for missed opportunities to use dialogue in nonfiction. Pay special attention to reports about crime, civic controversies, and the courtroom.

3. Develop your ear for dialogue. With a notebook in hand, sit in a public space, such as a mall or an airport lounge. Eavesdrop on nearby conversations and jot down some notes on what it would take to capture that speech in a story.

4. Read the work of a contemporary playwright, such as Tony Kushner. Read the dialogue aloud with friends, and discuss to what extent it sounds like real speech or seems artificial.

5. Interview two people about an important conversation they had years ago. Try to re-create the dialogue to their satisfaction. Speak to them separately, then bring them together.

—◄○►—

# Reveal traits of character.

*Show character-istics through scenes,*
*details, and dialogue.*

In a wonderful essay, Nora Ephron describes a lady who hopes to become the winner of a national baking competition:

> Edna Buckley, who was fresh from representing New York State at the National Chicken Cooking contest, where her recipe for fried chicken in a batter of beer, cheese, and crushed pretzels had gone down to defeat, brought with her a lucky handkerchief, a lucky horseshoe, a lucky dime for her shoe, a potholder with the Pillsbury Poppin' Fresh Doughboy on it, an Our Blessed Lady pin, and all of her jewelry, including a silver charm also in the shape of the doughboy. (from *Crazy Salad*)

I love what is *not* in this sentence: vague character adjectives, words like *superstitious* or *quirky* or *obsessive*. Ephron's litany of details opens Edna Buckley up for inspection. Cloudy adjectives would close her down.

A story in *USA Today* described a teenage surfer in Hawaii who lost her arm in a shark attack. It began like this:

> Bethany Hamilton has always been a compassionate child. But since the 14-year-old Hawaiian surfing sensation lost her left arm in a shark attack on Halloween, her compassion has deepened.

This opening fell flat, I think, because of the adjective "compassionate." Too often, writers turn abstractions into adjectives to define character. One writer tells us the shopkeeper was *enthusiastic,* or that the lawyer was *passionate* in his closing argument, or that the schoolgirls were *popular.* Some adjectives — *ashen, blond,* and *winged* — help us see. But adjectives such as *enthusiastic* are abstract nouns in disguise.

The reader who encounters character adjectives screams silently for examples, for evidence: "Don't just *tell* me, Ms. Writer, that Super Surfer Girl is compassionate. *Show* me." And, to her credit, she does.

Jill Lieber describes how Bethany Hamilton, from her hospital bed, "tearfully insisted" that the fifteen-hundred-pound tiger shark that attacked her "not be harmed." Later the girl meets with a blind psychologist and offers him the charitable donations she is receiving "to fund an operation to restore his sight."

> And in December, Hamilton touched more hearts when, on a media tour of New York City, she suddenly removed her ski jacket and gave it to a homeless girl sitting on a subway grate in Times Square. Wearing only a tank top, Hamilton then canceled a shopping spree, saying she already had too many things.

*Now* I see. That girl really *is* compassionate.

The best writers create moving pictures of people, images that reveal their characteristics and aspirations, their hopes and fears. Writing for the *New York Times,* Isabel Wilkerson describes a mother in desperate fear for the safety of her children, but avoids adjectives such as *desperate* and *fearful.* Instead she shows us a woman preparing her children for school:

> Then she sprays them. She shakes an aerosol can and sprays their coats, their heads, their tiny outstretched hands. She sprays them back and front to protect them as they go off to school, facing bullets and gang recruiters and a crazy dangerous world. It is a special religious oil that smells like drugstore perfume, and the children

shut their eyes tight as she sprays them long and furious so they will come back to her, alive and safe, at day's end.

By re-creating this moment, Wilkerson leads us into the world of a struggling family, offering us the opportunity for sympathy. The scenic evidence is supported by the spoken words of the children:

> These are the rules for Angela Whitiker's children, recounted at the Formica-top dining room table:
>
> "Don't stop off playing," Willie said.
>
> "When your hear shooting, don't stand around — run," Nicholas said.
>
> "Because a bullet don't have no eyes," the two boys shouted.
>
> "She pray for us every day," Willie said.

Writing for the *Maine Sunday Telegram,* Barbara Walsh introduces us to a group of girls facing the social pressures of middle school. The story begins at a school dance in a gym that "smells of peach and watermelon perfume, cheap aftershave, cinnamon Tic Tacs, bubble gum." Groups of girls dance in tight circles, adjusting their hair and moving to the music.

> "I loooove this song," Robin says.
>
> Robin points to a large group of 20 boys and girls clustered near the DJ.
>
> "Theeeey are the populars, and we're nooot," she shouts over the music.
>
> "We're the middle group," Erin adds. "You've just got to form your own group and dance."

"But if you dance with someone that isn't too popular, it's not cool," Robin says. "You lose points," she adds, thrusting her thumbs down.

What is this story about? The words I would choose lead me up the ladder of abstraction: Adolescence. Self-consciousness. Peer pressure. Social status. Anxiety. Self-expression. Vulnerability. Groupthink. How much better for us as readers to see and hear these truths through the actions of interesting young women, with their authentic adolescent vowel sounds, than from the abstracting lips of sociologists.

## WORKSHOP

1. Some writers talk about doing research until they arrive at a dominant impression, something they can express in a single sentence. For example, "The mother of the cheerleader is overbearing and controlling." They may never write that sentence. Instead, they try to re-create for the reader the evidence that led them to this conclusion. Try out this method on some of your stories.

2. Listen to stories reported and written for National Public Radio. Pay attention to the voices of story subjects and sources. What character traits do they reveal in their speech? How would you render that speech in print?

3. Sit with notebook ready in a public place: a mall, a cafeteria, a sports stadium. Watch people's behavior, appearance, and speech. Write down the character adjectives that come to mind: *obnoxious, affectionate, caring, confused.* Now write down the specific details that led you to those conclusions.

◄○►

# Put odd and interesting things next to each other.

*Help the reader learn from contrast.*

At its best, the study of literature helps us understand what reading scholar Frank Smith describes as the "grammar of stories." Such was the case on my first encounter with Emma Bovary, the provincial French heroine with the tragically romantic imagination. I remember my amazement at reading the scene in which author Gustave Flaubert describes the seduction of the married and bored Madame Bovary by the cad Rodolphe Boulanger. The setting is an agricultural fair. In a scene both poignant and hilarious, Flaubert switches from the flirtatious language of the lover to the calls of animal husbandry in the background.

I remember it as a back-and-forth between such dialogue as "I tried to make myself leave a thousand times, but still I followed you" and the sounds of "Manure for sale!" Or "I will have a place in your thoughts and your life, won't I?" and "Here's the prize for the best pigs!"

Back and forth, back and forth, the juxtaposition exposes to the reader, but not to our heroine, Rodolphe's true intentions. *Ironic juxtaposition* is the fancy term for what happens when two disparate things are placed side by side, each commenting on the other.

This effect can work in music, in the visual arts, and in poetry:

Let us go then, you and I,
When the evening is spread out against the sky
Like a patient etherized upon a table;

So begins "The Love Song of J. Alfred Prufrock," a poem in which T. S. Eliot juxtaposes the romantic image of the evening sky with the sickly metaphor of anesthesia. The tension between those images sets the tone for everything that follows. Eliot died in 1965, my junior year in Catholic high school, and a group of us celebrated the event by naming our rock band after the poet. We were called "T. S. and the Eliots," and our motto was "Music with Soul," our sophomoric attempt at ironic juxtaposition.

How about *Buffy the Vampire Slayer*? Valley girl becomes scourge of demons.

The coupling of unlikely elements is often the occasion for humor, broad and subtle. In *The Producers,* for example, Mel Brooks creates a musical called "Springtime for Hitler," starring a hippy Führer, and featuring Busby Berkeley–style dancers who form the image of a swastika.

Moving from the grotesquely comic to the deadly serious, consider this introduction to the *Philadelphia Inquirer*'s story of the nuclear accident at Three Mile Island:

4:07 a.m. March 28, 1979.

Two pumps fail. Nine seconds later, 69 boron rods smash down into the hot core of unit two, a nuclear reactor on Three Mile Island. The rods work. Fission in the reactor stops.

But it is already too late.

What will become America's worst commercial nuclear disaster has begun.

What follows is a catalog of terrible truths that officials will learn, along with harrowing details: "Nuclear workers playing Frisbee outside a plant gate because they were locked out but not warned of the radiation beaming from the plant's walls." The suspense that builds from those first short sentences reaches a peak when the failed nuclear reactor produces radiation that bombards workers playing Frisbee. Radiation meets Frisbee. Surprising juxtaposition.

In some cases, the effect of juxtaposition can be accomplished by a few words embedded in a narrative. The narrator of the dark crime novel *The Postman Always Rings Twice* lays out the plot to murder his girlfriend's husband:

> We played it just like we would tell it. It was about ten o'clock at night, and we had closed up, and the Greek was in the bathroom, putting on his Saturday night wash. I was to take the water up to my room, get ready to shave, and then remember I had left the car out. I was to go outside, and stand by to give her one on the horn if somebody came. She was to wait till she heard him in the tub, go in for a towel, and clip him from behind with a blackjack I had made for her out of a sugar bag with ball bearings wadded down in the end.

James M. Cain creates a double effect in this passage, placing the innocent "sugar bag" between the mechanical "ball bearings" and the criminal "blackjack." A sack for sugar loses its sweetness when converted into a murder weapon.

Olivia Judson, a science writer, uses this technique to tweak our interest in what could be a stultifying subject, the female green spoon worm:

> The green spoon worm has one of the most extreme size differences known to exist between male and female, the male being 200,000 times smaller than his mate. Her life span is a couple of years. His is only a couple of months — and he spends his short life inside her reproductive tract, regurgitating sperm through his

mouth to fertilize her eggs. More ignominious still, when he was first discovered, he was thought to be a nasty parasitic infestation. (from *Seed* magazine)

The author's point of view is a sly wink, the humiliation of the minuscule male sea creature serving as an emblem for his crude and increasingly miniaturized human counterpart. The juxtaposition is between worm sex and human sex.

We would expect to see weird juxtapositions in the work of ironists and satirists, and so it goes with this passage about a baby killed at Christmas in a laundry room dryer:

> The shock and horror that followed Don's death are something I would rather not recount: Calling our children to report the news, watching the baby's body, small as a loaf of bread, as it was zipped into a heavy plastic bag — these images have nothing to do with the merriment of Christmas, and I hope my mention of them will not dampen your spirits at this, the most special and glittering time of the year. (from *Holidays on Ice*)

This conflation of offbeat images and ideas — the juxtaposition of a bizarre murder with the expectation of Yuletide frivolity — is David Sedaris at his best.

Notice that I drew my examples from fiction, poetry, musical comedy, journalism, science writing, and satire — proof of the utility and versatility of this tool.

## WORKSHOP

1. Feature photographers often see startling visual details in juxtaposition: a street person wearing a corsage, a massive sumo wrestler holding a tiny child. Keep your eyes open for such visual images and imagine how you would represent them in your writing.

2. Reread your own work to see if surprising juxtapositions

are hiding inside. Can you revise your work to take better advantage of these opportunities?

3. Now that you have a name for this technique, you will begin to recognize its use more often in literature, theater, movies, music, and journalism. Make a mental note of such examples. And look for them in real life as you research your writing.

―◄o►―

# Foreshadow dramatic events and powerful conclusions.

*Plant important clues early.*

The creepy experience of my youth was reading Shirley Jackson's "The Lottery," a short, short story that begins in innocence: "The morning of June 27th was clear and sunny, with the fresh warmth of a full-summer day; the flowers were blossoming profusely and the grass was richly green." What a splendid day to conduct the annual village lottery, I must have thought, and who will be the winner? And what will they win?

The "winner," of course, turns out to be Tessie Hutchinson, whose prize is to be stoned to death, a scapegoat to the villagers' blind adherence to tradition: " 'It isn't fair, it isn't right,' Mrs. Hutchinson screamed, and then they were upon her." Those words still crawl up my spine, years after I first encountered them.

Yet, the "surprise" stoning is foreshadowed right there in the story's first few paragraphs: "Bobby Martin had already stuffed his pockets full of stones, and the other boys soon followed his example, selecting the smoothest and roundest stones." Surely, I thought, those stones must be instruments in some boyhood game. Little did I know they prefigured the story's unthinkable finale.

Not long ago, I saw a movie that reminded me of the power

of foreshadowing. Clues planted early in the story offered what a dictionary definition describes as "vague advance indications" of important future events.

In *Harry Potter and the Prisoner of Azkaban,* terrible events are reversed at the end when Hermione reveals to Harry her ability to travel back in time by means of a charm she wears around her neck, a time turner. On first viewing, the plot twist comes as a surprise. Watching the film a second time, I noticed how often the director makes reference to time, especially in visual images of huge pendulums and giant clockworks.

For novels and movies, it may require several readings or viewings to appreciate all the effects of foreshadowing. The technique becomes more transparent in works of shorter length. Consider this narrative poem, "Uncle Jim," by Peter Meinke:

> What the children remember about Uncle Jim
> is that on the train to Reno to get divorced
> so he could marry again
> he met another woman and woke up in California.
> It took him seven years to untangle that dream
> but a man who could sing like Uncle Jim
> was bound to get in scrapes now and then:
> he expected it and we expected it.
>
> Mother said, It's because he was the middle child,
> And Father said, Yeah, where there's trouble
> Jim's in the middle.
>
> When he lost his voice he lost all of it
> to the surgeon's knife and refused the voice box
> they wanted to insert. In fact he refused
> almost everything. *Look, they said,*
> *It's up to you. How many years*
> *do you want to live?* and Uncle Jim
> held up one finger.
> The middle one.

The poet gives us a verse with a punch line, set up by the fore-shadowing in the middle stanza. Jim's the middle child, always in the middle of trouble, so why not at the end flash that middle finger?

Foreshadowing in fiction? Yes. In film? Yes. In narrative poetry? Yes. In journalism? Let's see.

In 1980 a huge oil tanker collided with a tall bridge near my hometown, destroying more than one thousand feet of the span, sending a bus and several cars two hundred feet to the bottom of Tampa Bay, killing more than thirty people. The late great Gene Miller of the *Miami Herald* was in town on another assignment and managed to find the driver of a car that skidded to a stop twenty-four inches from the jagged edge. Here is his memorable lead, a sidebar to the main story:

> Richard Hornbuckle, auto dealer, golfer, Baptist, came within two feet Friday of driving his yellow Buick Skylark off the Sunshine Skyway Bridge into Tampa Bay.

That simple sentence takes twenty-five words, but each one advances the story. First, Miller takes advantage of the protagonist's unusual name — Hornbuckle — with its auto imagery. This will turn out to be the story of an auto dealer driving a used car with good brakes. And Miller, a master of detail, gets good mileage out of "yellow Buick Skylark." "Yellow" goes with "Sunshine," and "Skylark" goes with "Skyway." He's playing with words.

But the real fun comes with those three nouns after the subject, for each foreshadows a thread of narrative in the story. "Auto dealer" sets up a description of Hornbuckle's work schedule and how he came to be at that spot on that day. "Golfer" prepares us for the crazy moment when — during his escape from the vehicle — Hornbuckle turns back to retrieve his golf clubs from the trunk. (He probably had a tee time later that day.) And "Baptist" makes way for a wry quote in which the reluctant believer turned survivor swears that he'll be in church the next morning. "Auto dealer, golfer, Baptist."

In dramatic literature, this technique inherits the name *Chekhov's Gun*. In a letter he penned in 1889, Russian playwright Anton Chekhov wrote: "One must not put a loaded rifle on the stage if no one is thinking of firing it."

I conclude with a strategy I call *Hitchcock's Leg of Lamb*. A 1958 episode of Alfred Hitchcock's mystery series told the story of a pregnant housewife who kills her cheating husband with a frozen leg of lamb, and then feeds the murder weapon to the investigating detectives. Written by Roald Dahl, the action in this dark comedy is prefigured in its title, "Lamb to the Slaughter."

## WORKSHOP

1. Do you ever violate the principle of Chekhov's Gun? Do you place seemingly significant elements high in your work that never come into play again?

2. Until now, you may not have noticed the technique of foreshadowing in movies, fiction, and dramatic literature. Now that you have a name for it, look for examples.

3. Foreshadowing can work not only in narrative forms, but also in persuasive writing. A good column or essay has a point, often revealed at the end. Which details can you place early to foreshadow your conclusion?

4. In nonfiction, literary effects must be researched or reported, not invented. In your next writing project, see if you can visualize the shape of an ending during your research. That way, you may be able to gather details to help foreshadow your ending.

---◄◦►---

# To generate suspense, use internal cliffhangers.

*To propel readers, make them wait.*

What makes a page-turner, an irresistible read, a story or book that you can't put down? One indispensable tool is the internal cliffhanger. This device leaves the reader in suspense, a word derived from the Latin *suspendere*, "to hang under." Suspense leaves the reader, and sometimes a character, hanging.

The immense popularity of the novel *The Da Vinci Code* comes not from Dan Brown's graceful prose style, but from a clever plot built on a series of cliffhangers. A small sample will demonstrate this simple but powerful effect:

• "As he fell, he thought for a moment he saw a pale ghost hovering over him, clutching a gun. Then everything went black."

• "Before Sophie and Teabing could respond, a sea of blue police lights and sirens erupted at the bottom of the hill and began snaking up the half-mile driveway.

"Teabing frowned. 'My friends, it seems we have a decision to make. And we'd better make it fast.' "

• "Langdon dialed zero, knowing that the next sixty seconds might answer a question that had been puzzling him all night."

• "Langdon felt shaky as he inched deeper into the circular room. This had to be the place."

Each of these examples ends a chapter, fueling the reader's desire to learn what happens next. So if you want to sell a gazillion books, learn how to craft the cliffhanger.

You don't need a cliff to write a good cliffhanger. In the memoir *Father Joe*, Tony Hendra describes a wise and benevolent priest who comforts and directs the young Hendra through a time of adolescent trouble. Here's the end of chapter three: "All of a sudden there was the sound of sandals squishing along the corridor and the swish of long skirts. The door opened. And there stood one of the oddest human beings I'd ever laid eyes on." Father Joe is not tied to a railroad track. The simple need to learn what he looks like drove me to the next chapter.

I found a great example of the internal cliffhanger in my own backyard. A page one story in the *St. Petersburg Times* described the struggle to keep desperate folks from jumping from the top of the Sunshine Skyway Bridge. This turns out to be a terrible problem, not just in St. Pete, but wherever a high, dramatic bridge lures the depressed and suicidal.

Here's the opening segment of the story by reporter Jamie Jones:

> The lonely young blond left church on a windy afternoon and drove to the top of the Sunshine Skyway Bridge.
>
> Wearing black pumps and a shiny black dress, she climbed onto the ledge and looked at the chilly blue waters 197 feet below. The wind seemed to nudge her. It's time, she thought.
>
> She raised her arms skyward and pushed off the edge. Two boaters watched as she began a swan dive into Tampa Bay.
>
> Halfway down, [she] wanted to turn back. I don't want to die, she thought.

A second later, she slammed into the water. It swallowed her, and then let her go. She broke through the surface, screaming.

I've wondered whether the reporter should have stopped the action at "She raised her arms skyward and pushed off the edge." But the effect is still strong, and the reporter organized the whole story that way. She divided the work into seven sections, each separated from the others by the visual marker of three black boxes. Each section has a bit of drama at the end, a reward for the reader, and a reason to plunge forward.

We don't think of the cliffhanger as an internal device. We associate it with serialized film or television adventures with big endings. The super-sized ones come at the end of a season and sustain your interest until the next, as in the famous "Who shot J. R.?" of *Dallas* fame. Think of it as the "to be continued" effect, and consider how much some of us resent waiting six months to find out what happens.

I stumbled on the internal cliffhanger by reading adventure books for young readers. I hold in my hand a reprint of the very first Nancy Drew mystery story, *The Secret of the Old Clock*. I quote from page 159, the conclusion of chapter XIX:

> Clutching the blanket and the clock tightly in her arms, Nancy Drew partly crawled and partly fell over objects as she struggled to get out of the truck before it was too late. She was afraid to think what would happen to her if the robbers discovered her in the van.

> Reaching the door, she leaped lightly to the floor. She could now hear heavy footsteps coming closer and closer.

> Nancy slammed the truck doors shut and searched wildly for the keys.

> "Oh, what did I do with them?" she thought frantically.

She saw that they had fallen from the door to the floor and snatched them up. Hurriedly inserting the right key in the lock, she secured the doors.

The deed was not accomplished a minute too soon. As Nancy wheeled about she distinctly heard the murmur of angry voices outside. The robbers were quarreling among themselves, and already someone was working at the fastening of the barn door.

Escape was cut off. Nancy felt that she was cornered.

"Oh, what shall I do?" she thought in despair.

There you have it, the internal cliffhanger, daring you to stop reading.

Think about it. This technique energizes every episode of every television drama. Even the so-called reality shows force us to sit through a commercial break to learn which character has been excommunicated. Any dramatic element that comes right before a break in the action is an internal cliffhanger.

## WORKSHOP

1. As you read novels and nonfiction books, notice what the author places at the ends of chapters. How do these elements drive you to turn the page — or not?

2. Pay attention to the narrative structure of television dramas. Writers of these shows often place dramatic elements just before the commercial breaks. Look for examples that work and for ones that fail to keep you intrigued.

3. If you write for a publication, consider what it would take to put a mini-cliffhanger near the end of a section, especially when the reader is asked to turn inside to another page.

4. If you write for a blog or Web site, consider what it would take to place a mini-cliffhanger at the end of the first screenful of text online so that readers could not resist a click or scroll.

—◄○►—

# Build your work around a key question.

*Stories need an engine, a question*
*that the action answers for the reader.*

Who done it? Guilty or not guilty? Who will win the race? Which man will she marry? Will the hero escape or die trying? Will the body be found? Good questions drive good stories.

This narrative strategy is so powerful that it needs a name, and Tom French gave it to me: he calls it the "engine" of the story. He defines the engine as the question the story answers for the reader. If the internal cliffhanger drives the reader from one section to the next, the engine moves the reader across the arc from beginning to end.

In the book *Driving Mr. Albert,* Michael Paterniti narrates a bizarre cross-country adventure, no ordinary road trip. His driving companion? The old medical examiner who dissected the corpse of Albert Einstein and kept the great man's brain in a jar for forty years. The three of them — writer, doctor, gray matter in the trunk — head west to meet Einstein's daughter. *Will the quirky old doctor finally give up the brain, which is his talisman and life's work?* That sentence never appears in the story but keeps the reader focused on the destination through the curious side trips along the way.

As I thought about this tool, I came across a story in my local newspaper about a man hired as a greeter at a new Wal-Mart:

Charles Burns has been waiting for weeks to say three words:

"Welcome to Wal-Mart!"

When the doors open this morning at St. Petersburg's first Wal-Mart Supercenter, Burns' face will be one of the first that shoppers see.

He is the greeter.

Because this amiable feature is written the day before the opening, we never see Charles Burns in action. He never greets anybody. As a result, there is no engine, not even a simple *How did his first day of greeting go?* or *What was the response from the first customer?* or *How did the experience match the expectation?*

In the same edition, I read a much more serious story about tsunami survivors in Sri Lanka:

> In the pediatric ward of the town hospital here, Sri Lanka's most celebrated tsunami orphan dozes, drools and, when he is in a foul mood, wails at the many visitors who crowd around his crib.

> His identity is unknown. His age, according to hospital staff, is between 4 and 5 months. He is simply and famously known as Baby No. 81, the 81st admission to the ward this year.

> Baby No. 81's awful burden is not in being unwanted, but in being wanted too much.

> So far, nine couples have claimed him as their own son.

This story, which first appeared in the *New York Times*, has a supercharged engine. If you are like me, the engine took the form of questions such as these: What will happen to Baby No. 81? Will we ever learn his name and identity? Who will wind up with

Baby No. 81, and why? How will they determine the true parents among conflicting claims?

To its credit, the story raises questions of its own, not just about what might happen next, but also about the story's higher meaning:

> Could it possibly be that nine couples honestly believe Baby No. 81 to be their flesh and blood? Could it be that childless parents are looking for a boon amid the disaster? Could it be that a photogenic baby boy has inspired a craving that a girl would not have? All these theories circulate on the streets of Kalmunai.

A story, especially one with subplots, can have mini-engines. In the movie *The Full Monty,* unemployed factory workers try to make money as male strippers. The engine is something like, will these odd-shaped men go all the way — and how will it bring them love and money? But here's what makes the story work: each man has something important at stake and is motivated by his own particular engine. Will the overweight guy restore the spark to his marriage? Will the skinny guy lose custody of his son? Will the old guy find a way to pay his debts?

When Jan Winburn served as editor at the *Baltimore Sun,* she helped her writers create a cast of characters for their stories by asking the question *Who has something at stake here?* The answer can lead to the creation of a story engine: Will the loser of the contest still get her wish?

I think of the story engine as a distant cousin of what Lajos Egri calls the "premise" of a story. "Everything has a purpose, or premise," he writes. For *Romeo and Juliet,* it is "Great love defies even death." For *Macbeth,* it is "Ruthless ambition leads to its own destruction." For *Othello,* it is "Jealousy destroys itself and the object of its love." The premise takes the question of the engine and turns it into a thematic statement. It can easily be converted back: Will Othello's jealousy destroy him and the woman he loves?

Tom French makes a distinction between the engine of the story and its theme:

> To me, the engine is this raw visceral power that drives the story and keeps the reader engaged. How the writer uses that engine — the ideas that we explore along the way, and the deeper themes we're hoping to illuminate — is a matter of choice. A good example: *Citizen Kane*. Its opening scene sets up one of the most famous story engines of all time, what is Rosebud? Yet the movie isn't about the sled, or even particularly about Kane's childhood. Still, the reporter's quest to unlock the riddle of the dying man's last word drives the story forward and keeps us watching as Orson Welles explores deeper themes of politics, democracy, America. The mystery of Rosebud drives us through what's essentially a civics lesson on the real nature of power.

Finally, we should note that some stories are driven not by *what* questions, but by *how*. We know before the opening credits that James Bond will conquer the villains and get the girl, but we are driven to know how. We imagine that the affable Ferris Bueller will not be punished for his truancy, but we delight in knowing how he will escape detection.

Good writers anticipate the reader's questions and answer them. Editors will keep lookout for holes in the story where key questions are left unanswered. Storytellers take these questions to a narrative level, creating in the reader a curiosity that can only be quenched by reaching the end.

## WORKSHOP

1. Review a collection of your recent work. See if you can find story engines, or at least potential story engines.

2. Look for stories that capture your attention. Does the story have an engine? If so, what is the question that the story answers for you?

3. Look for engines in films and television narratives. Does an episode of *I Love Lucy* have an engine? How about an episode of *Seinfeld*, which is supposed to be about "nothing"? How about one of the many police procedure dramas?

4. As you read newspaper reports, look for underdeveloped stories that might benefit from the energy of an engine.

—<o>—

# Place gold coins along the path.

*Reward the reader with high points,*
*especially in the middle.*

How do you keep a reader moving through your story? We have described three techniques that do the trick: foreshadowing, cliffhangers, and story engines. Don Fry suggests yet another with this parable: Imagine you are walking on a narrow path through a deep forest. You stroll a mile, and there at your feet you find a gold coin. You pick it up and put it in your pocket. You walk another mile, and, sure enough, you see another gold coin. What will you do next? You walk another mile in search of another coin, of course.

Like our walker in the forest, the reader makes predictions about what lies down the road. When readers encounter boring and technical information, especially at the beginning, they will expect more boring matter below. When readers read chronological narratives, they wonder what will happen next.

Think of a gold coin as any bit that rewards the reader. A good start is its own reward, and crafty writers know enough to put something shiny at the end, a final reward, an invitation for readers to return to their work. But what about the territory between beginning and end? With no gold coins for motivation, the reader may drift out of the forest. Yet I've never met a writer, even a great one, who was praised for a brilliant middle — which is why the middle receives so little attention.

"The easiest thing for a reader to do," argued famed editor Barney Kilgore, "is to quit reading."

A gold coin can appear as a small scene or anecdote: "A big buck antelope squirms under a fence and sprints over the plain, hoofs drumming powerfully. 'Now that's one fine sight,' murmurs a cowboy."

It might appear as a startling fact: "Lightning . . . is much feared by any mounted man caught on the open plain, and many cowboys have been killed by it."

It can appear as a telling quote: " 'Most of the real cowboys I know,' says Mr. Miller, 'have been dead for a while.' "

These three gold coins appeared in a prize-winning story on the dying culture of the cowboy, written by Bill Blundell for the *Wall Street Journal,* a newspaper that takes the act of rewarding the reader seriously — and sometimes humorously.

A commonplace of Shakespeare studies is the importance of act 3. The first two acts build toward a moment of powerful insight or action; the last two resolve the tension that forms midway through the play. In other words, the Bard places a huge gold coin right in the middle of his plays. I tested this idea against Shakespeare's greatest tragedies and found the pattern fulfilled. In act 3 of *Hamlet,* the young prince crafts a play within a play that reveals the treachery of the king; in *Othello,* the title character is persuaded by the treacherous Iago that his bride has been unfaithful; in *King Lear,* the great ancient monarch is stripped to his bare essence and left howling in a hurricane.

Armed with evidence that there's gold in the middle, I undertook a literary experiment. I walked over to my bookshelf and picked out the first great work of literature that caught my eye, *Huckleberry Finn* by Mark Twain. My Riverside edition has forty-two chapters, so I thumbed to the middle — chapter XXI — to see if the author had buried some gold. I was not disappointed. Huck narrates the hilarious story of two phony Shakespearean actors who take their act around the territory, butchering the

Bard with outrageous misrenderings. So Hamlet's most famous soliloquy turns out to be a mishmash of familiar phrases: "To be or not to be; that is the bare bodkin." I wonder if it's more than coincidence that Twain uses these corny players (in the middle of the novel) to parody *Hamlet*'s central scene.

Which leads me to my favorite gold coin of all time, a passage from a 1984 story written by Peter Rinearson for the *Seattle Times*. The gold coin appeared in a long chapter in a long series about the creation of a new airliner, the Boeing 757. The chapter on engineering, for example, included endless details about the passenger door, how it contained five hundred parts and was "held together by 5,900 rivets."

Just when my interest began to fade, I came across a passage that described how engineers tested the integrity of cockpit windows, which are often hit by birds:

> Boeing is a little touchy about the subject of chicken tests, and points out they are required by the FAA. Here's what happens:
>
> A live 4-pound chicken is anesthetized and placed in a flimsy plastic bag to reduce aerodynamic drag. The bagged bird is put in a compressed-air gun.
>
> The bird is fired at the jetliner window at 360 knots and the window must withstand the impact. It is said to be a very messy test.
>
> The inch-thick glass, which includes two layers of plastic, needn't come out unscathed. But it must not puncture. The test is repeated under various circumstances — the window is cooled by liquid nitrogen, or the chicken is fired into the center of the window or at its edge. "We give Boeing an option," Berven joked. "They can either use a 4-pound chicken at 200 miles an hour or a 200-pound chicken at 4 miles an hour."

No one who reads about the chicken test thinks about air travel or Colonel Sanders the same way again.

While the authors of books and screenplays know the value of dramatic and comic high points in a story, journalists have a disadvantage. Their work is so top heavy that even an eager editor will do the wrong thing for the right reason.

"That's a great quote," says the admiring editor to the writer. "Let's move it up."

"Readers will learn a lot from that anecdote. Let's move it up." And so it goes. Moving up the good bits honors the material but may dishonor the story. The result is bait and switch. The reader winds up with three or four nifty paragraphs, followed by the toxic waste that drifts to the bottom.

## WORKSHOP

1. Think about the strategy of the gold coins. Review your recent works to see if they are top heavy. Look for missed opportunities to create a more balanced structure.

2. Carry the concept of the gold coins into your reading and movie watching. Study the structure of stories, looking for the strategic placement of dramatic or comic high points.

3. Take a draft you are working on and identify the gold coins. Draw a star next to any story element that shines. Now study their placement and consider moving them around.

4. See if you can recognize gold coins during your research. When you see one or hear one, report it thoroughly so it can have the best possible effect in your story.

5. Find the geographic middle in some pieces of your writing. Is there a gold coin in sight?

# Tool 33

◄○►

# Repeat, repeat, and repeat.

*Purposeful repetition links the parts.*

Repetition works in writing, but only if you intend it. Repeating key words, phrases, and story elements creates a rhythm, a pace, a structure, a wavelength that reinforces the central theme of the work. Such repetition works in music, in literature, in advertising, in humor, in political speech and rhetoric, in teaching, in homilies, in parental lectures — even in this sentence, where the word "in" is repeated ten times.

Repetition gives texture to conversation and dialogue, lending dramatic literature the feeling that real people speak in a real world:

ROY: I'm dying, Joe. Cancer.

JOE: Oh my God.

ROY: Please. Let me finish.

Few people know this and I'm telling you this only because. . . . I'm not afraid of *death*. What can death bring that I haven't faced? I've lived; *life* is the worst. *(Gently mocking himself)* Listen to me, I'm a philosopher.

Joe. You *must* do this. You must must must. Love; that's a *trap*. Responsibility; that's a trap too. Like a father to a son I tell you this: Life is full of horror; *nobody* escapes, nobody; save yourself. *Whatever* pulls on you, whatever needs from you, threatens you. Don't be *afraid;* people are so afraid; don't be afraid to *live* in the raw wind, naked, alone. . . . Learn at least this: What you are capable of. Let nothing stand in your way.

This remarkable dialogue comes from Tony Kushner's epic play *Angels in America.* To my ear, the repetition makes it seem real. And consider the words the playwright chooses to repeat for emphasis in a passage of only 126 words: "death," "life," "must," "trap," "nobody," "whatever," "afraid," "live."

Repetition can work in sentences and paragraphs, as well as across the longer stretches of a story. Consider this scene from Maya Angelou's memoir *I Know Why the Caged Bird Sings:*

> His twang jogged in the brittle air. From the side of the Store, Bailey and I heard him say to Momma, "Annie, tell Willie he better lay low tonight. A crazy nigger messed with a white lady today. Some of the boys'll be coming over here later." Even after the slow drag of years, I remember the sense of fear which filled my mouth with hot, dry air, and made my body light.

> The "boys"? Those cement faces and eyes of hate that burned the clothes off you if they happened to see you lounging on the main street downtown on Saturday. Boys? It seemed that youth had never happened to them. Boys? No, rather men who were covered with graves' dust and age without beauty or learning. The ugliness and rottenness of old abominations.

The author fills this passage with interesting language, from dialogue expressed in dialect to phrases of biblical connotation. The repetition of "boys" holds it together.

Writers use repetition as a tool of persuasion, few as skillfully as Michael Gartner, who, in a distinguished and varied journalism career, won a Pulitzer Prize for editorial writing. Consider this excerpt from "Tattoos and Freedom":

> Let's talk about tattoos.
>
> We haven't seen the arms of Jackson Warren, the food-service worker at Iowa State University, but they do sound repulsive. A swastika on one, KKK on the other.
>
> Ugh.
>
> That's obnoxious.
>
> The administrators at the university think so, too, so in response to a student's complaint they've "temporarily reassigned" Warren to a job where he won't be in contact with the general public.
>
> Ugh.
>
> That's outrageous. (from the *Daily Tribune*, Ames, Iowa)

Gartner's repetition of "ugh" and "That's obnoxious/outrageous" frames the argument for protection of free speech, even when that speech is expressed in a hateful way.

> Remember the flag burners in Texas? The Nazi marchers in Skokie? The war protesters everywhere? Protected citizens, one and all. Obnoxious, sometimes. Outrageous, sometimes. Despicable, sometimes.
>
> But never unspeakable.

The pattern throughout is repetition, repetition, repetition, flavored by variation. At the end of the editorial, Gartner answers the question of what message the presence of the tattoo man sends to students on campus, many of whom would find the tattoos repugnant:

> The message you're giving is clear:

> This is a school that believes in free speech.

> This is a school that protects dissent.

> This is a school that cherishes America.

> That's what Iowa State officials should be saying.

> For Jackson Warren, bedecked in symbols of hate, should himself be a symbol of freedom.

As we saw in Tool 20, the number of examples has meaning, and so does the number of repetitions. Three gives us a sense of the whole, while two creates comparison and contrast, symbols of hate versus symbol of freedom.

For Gartner, repetition is never accidental. "It's the refrain," he told Chip Scanlan,

> the rhythmic refrain with a different tag on it each time. It's almost a musical device. I love Broadway musicals and have always thought I could write a musical. Couldn't write the music, but I could write the lyrics because I like word play and rhymes, rhythms, and beats, and cadences. Sometimes I think these editorials are the lyrics to a song that has never been written.

In the hands of master teachers and poets, repetition has a power transcending the rhetorical, ascending to the level of myth and scripture. These words, for example, from the book *Night* by Elie Wiesel, are attached to a wall of the United States Holocaust Memorial Museum:

Never shall I forget that night, the first night in camp, which has turned my life into one long night, seven times cursed and seven times sealed. Never shall I forget that smoke. Never shall I forget the little faces of the children, whose bodies I saw turned into wreaths of smoke beneath a silent blue sky.

Never shall I forget those flames which consumed my faith forever.

Never shall I forget that nocturnal silence which deprived me, for all eternity, of the desire to live. Never shall I forget those moments which murdered my God and my soul and turned my dreams to dust. Never shall I forget these things, even if I am condemned to live as long as God Himself. Never.

Repetition can be so powerful, in fact, that it can threaten to call attention to itself, overshadowing the message of the story. If you're worried about too much repetition, apply this little test: Delete all the repetition and read the passage aloud without it. Repeat the key element once. Repeat it again. Your voice and ear will let you know when you've gone too far.

## WORKSHOP

1. Understand the difference between repetition and redundancy. The first is useful, designed to create a specific effect. The latter is useless, words wasted. Read your own work, looking for examples of both repetition and redundancy. What happens when you eliminate redundancy but reinforce repetition?

2. Read through an anthology of historical speeches and look for repetition. Make a list of the reasons the authors use repetition, starting with: to help us remember, to build an argument, to underscore emotion.

3. Try rewriting the passage by Elie Wiesel. For the sake of the

exercise, eliminate as many uses of "never" as you can without altering the meaning. Now read both the original version and your revision aloud. Think about what you've discovered.

4. Repetition does not have to be highly rhetorical. For example, you can mention or quote a character three times in a story, at the beginning, in the middle, and near the end, to chain the elements together. Look for examples of this style of repetition in news stories.

5. British author John Ruskin advised: "Say all you have to say in the fewest possible words, or your reader will be sure to skip them; and in the plainest possible words or he will certainly misunderstand them." Using the standards of "fewest" and "plainest," evaluate the repetition in the works cited above.

-<o>-

# Write from different cinematic angles.

*Turn your notebook into a camera.*

Before there was cinema, writers wrote cinematically. Influenced by the visual arts — by portraits and tapestries — authors have long understood how to shift their focus in and out to capture both character and landscape.

Many authors now write books with movies in mind, but cinematic techniques can be traced to the earliest expression of English literature. A thousand years ago, the unnamed poet who composed the epic *Beowulf* knew how to write cinematically. He could pull back the lens to establish heroic settings of land and sea; and he could move in close to see the jeweled fingers of the queen or the demonic light in a monster's eyes.

In our time, the epic poet has been replaced by authors such as David Sedaris, who grew up with the movies and sees the world through the lens of satire:

> Halloween fell on a Saturday that year, and by the time my mother took us to the store, all the good costumes were gone. My sisters dressed as witches and I went as a hobo. I'd looked forward to going in disguise to the Tomkeys' door, but they were off at the lake, and their house was dark. Before leaving, they had left a coffee can full of gumdrops on the front porch, alongside a sign

reading DON'T BE GREEDY. In terms of Halloween candy, individual gumdrops were just about as low as you could get. This was evidenced by the large number of them floating in an adjacent dog bowl. It was disgusting to think that this was what a gumdrop might look like in your stomach, and it was insulting to be told not to take too much of something you didn't really want in the first place. (from *Dress Your Family in Corduroy and Denim*)

In that single paragraph, I measure at least four different distances from the author's camera to the subject matter. The first is a quick shot of the children in their Halloween garb. The next is an image of the darkened house. The next one gets close enough for us to read the sign. Closer still are the gumdrops in the dog bowl. And perhaps we can add an X-ray image of nasty candy floating in a kid's tummy.

I learned the technique of reporting cinematically from my friend David Finkel, who covered the war in Kosovo in 1999 for the *Washington Post*. Finkel creates verbal cinema in describing refugees so needy that the act of helping them sparks a kind of warfare:

One of the volunteers picks up a loaf of bread and tosses it blindly. There is no chance it will hit the ground. There are too many people watching its flight, packed too tightly. Out goes another loaf, and another, and hundreds of arms suddenly stretch skyward, fingers extended and waving.

In this paragraph, Finkel begins with a close shot of one worker and then moves the camera back so we can see hundreds of arms. The crowd grows out of control, and Finkel focuses on one woman.

"For children. For children," a woman is shouting, arms out, trying to reach the cart. She is wearing earrings, a headband and a sweater, and when she can't reach the cart she brings her hands to her head and covers her ears because behind her is her daughter, perhaps 8, holding on to her, getting crushed, screaming.

And behind her is another girl, 10 perhaps, wearing a pink jacket decorated with drawings of cats and stars and flowers and now mud. She has red hair. There is mud in her hair.

Simple descriptions of standard camera angles should help you imagine how to use your "word cameras" for a variety of effects:

• *Aerial view.* The writer looks down on the world, as if standing atop a skyscraper or viewing the ground from a blimp. Example: "Hundreds and hundreds of black South African voters stood for hours on long, sandy serpentine lines waiting to cast their ballots for the first time."

• *Establishing shot.* The writer stands back to capture the setting in which action takes place, describing the world that the reader is about to enter, sometimes creating a mood for the story. Example: "Within seconds, as dusty clouds rose over the school grounds, their great widths suggesting blasts of terrifying force, bursts of rifle fire began to sound, quickly building to a sustained and rolling roar."

• *Middle distance.* The camera moves closer to the action, close enough to see the key players and their interaction. This is the common distance for most stories written for the newspaper. Example: "Scores of hostages survived, staggering from the school even as intense gunfire sputtered and grenades exploded around them. Many were barely dressed, their faces strained with fear and exhaustion, their bodies bloodied by shrapnel and gunshots."

• *Close-up.* The camera gets in the face of the subject, close enough to detect anger, fear, dread, sorrow, irony, the full range of emotions. Example: "His brow furrowed and the crow's feet deepened as he struggled to understand. . . . The man pulled at the waistband of his beige work pants and scratched his sunaged face. He stared at her, stalling for time as he tried to understand, but afraid to say he didn't."

• *Extreme close-up.* This writer focuses on an important detail that would be invisible from a distance: the pinky ring on the mobster's finger, the date circled on the wall calendar, the can of beer atop a police car. Example: "The hand of the cancer-care nurse scooped the dead angel fish out of the office aquarium. Patients at this clinic had enough on their minds. They didn't need another reminder of mortality."

Years ago I attended an outdoor concert in which the punk band the Ramones performed in a courtyard adjacent to a Florida retirement hotel. It was quite a scene. Down below, young fans sported turquoise Mohawk haircuts. Up above, blue-haired ladies stared out of windows, thinking the world had come to an end. A young writer sent to review the concert stood in one place for two hours with his notebook in his pocket. I fought the urge to knock him out and steal his notebook. He should have been exploring the territory like a photographer, seeing the event from down in the mosh pit and then up on the rooftop.

## WORKSHOP

1. Read selections of your recent work, paying attention to the distance between you and the story subjects. Look for your tendencies. Do you move the camera around? Or do you settle for a safe middle distance?

2. Changing camera distance and angle lies at the heart of cinematic art. Watch a favorite movie with a friend, paying attention to the camera work. Discuss how you would describe certain scenes if you had to write them for print.

3. When out in the field doing research, take a disposable camera or cell phone camera with you. Your goal is not to take publishable photos but to keep your eyes open. Be sure to take photos from different distances and angles. Review these before you write.

4. The next time you write about an event, change your vantage point. View the scene from close up and far back, from in front of the stage and behind it.

1. A woman finds a television
   not hers.
2. The woman walks down the str
   who cry out to her.
3. Another woman stands in th
   through her stuff.
4. " 'My cat is alive!' one man can
5. Another man emerges from h
   his guitar.
6. A distraught woman is comfor
7. A woman finds blistered photo
   a neighbor's patio.
8. A woman takes cell phone calls
   ing about their property.

These are moments of real life, dra
and ordered by a skillful young wri
gives them meaning and special po

WORKS

1. The next time you do fie
scenes you witness. Record these s
can re-create them for the reader.

2. As you invent scenes for fi
dramatic dialogue that can help re

3. Try an exercise created by
friends or students, view an inter
(French favors Vermeer). Althoug
writer must place details in an or
Write a scene describing each ima

4. Learn sequencing from care
vorite movie. Hit the pause button
lines up the scenes. How is meani

---

paragraphs — you build it
each changing something
the story inexorably and re

From childhood, we inl
literature and news reports
from movies and television
announcements, from our
are *mimetic,* to use an old-f
tations of real life.

The best writers work h
most interesting moments
(act 3, scene 2) directs the
scenes so realistic that the
murderous king: "Suit the a
tion, with this special obser
esty of nature." Anything e
melancholy prince, takes aw
which is "to hold . . . the n
mains a powerful metaphor
journalist. The writer's goa
here and now, so that reade
the job of the writer is not
them. These scenes, these
placed in a meaningful orde

You may think that t
chronological. But scenes c
time, from one side of a stre
balance parallel narrative li
the criminal to the cop. Sc
ahead.

One of the most arrest
ida hurricane season of 2
Nguyen of the *St. Petersb*
aftermath of Hurricane Iva
perience of folks returning

---

◄◦►

# Report and write for scenes.

*Then align them in a meaningful sequence.*

Tom Wolfe argues that realism, in fiction and nonfiction, is built on "scene-by-scene construction, telling the story by moving from scene to scene and resorting as little as possible to sheer historical narrative." This requires, according to Wolfe's manifesto in *The New Journalism,* "extraordinary feats of reporting," so that writers "actually witness the scenes in other people's lives."

That advice was offered more than forty years ago, but adherence to it still makes eyewitness storytelling seem new.

BAGHDAD, Iraq — On a cold, concrete slab, a mosque caretaker washed the body of 14-year-old Arkan Daif for the last time.

With a cotton swab dipped in water, he ran his hand across Daif's olive corpse, dead for three hours but still glowing with life. He blotted the rose-red shrapnel wounds on the soft skin of Daif's right arm and right ankle with the poise of practice. Then he scrubbed his face scabbed with blood, left by a cavity torn in the back of Daif's skull.

The men in the Imam Ali mosque stood somberly waiting to bury a boy who, in the words of his father, was "like a flower." Haider

Kathim, the caretaker, aske
What have they done?"

This is the Pulitzer Prize–wi
ering the war in Iraq for the
immersion journalism, get
scene after bloody scene.

Scenes can be witnessed
also be remembered, as in th
Ephron:

> It is September, just before
> about to enter the seventh
> each other all summer. . . .
> my jeans and father's shirt
> with the socks falling into
> take a deep breath . . . a you
> and she has a waist and h
> straight skirt, an article of
> will be unable to wear unti
> drops, and suddenly I am
> my breath sobbing. My bes
> ahead without me and dot
> *Salad*)

The scene is the basic unit
time and space created by tl
viewer. What we gain from
perience. We were there on
*are* there.

"As the atom is the sm
novelist Holly Lisle on her

> so the scene is the smallest
> est bit of fiction that cor
> You don't build a story o

destruction for the first time. It be
simple scene:

> They waited for days in the hot sun
> sheriff's deputies, straining for any gl

Because of the danger, authorities
elaboration of the scene:

> They brought coolers and portable c
> fine china. They warned each other a
> through the rubble because of the sn

In another scene they confront the

> "Why won't you let us in?" they shou

Bulldozers clear debris from the n
of scenes reveals the emotional as v

> The residents who had just been j
> find walked along Grand Lagoon B

> Five houses in, they began to weep.

> Women wailed inside cars. Teenag
> trucks with their hands covering th

The camera moves closer.

> Carla Godwin quietly walked do
> neighbors lifted roofing from bi
> plates. "We don't even have a din
> sobbed. "I don't know where it is. I

A sequence of tiny scenes follows

> crystal-clear memory for Ruby into old age: "Oh, my children," he
> cried out, nearly overcome with emotion, and embraced them.

Lemann then pulls the camera back and up from this emotional
moment. His next perspective, from high atop the ladder of abstraction, draws on history, sociology, anthropology, ethnog-
raphy:

> Americans are imbued with the notion that social systems pro-
> ceed from ideas, because that is what happened at the founding of
> our country. The relationship of society and ideas can work the
> other way around, though: people can create social systems first
> and then invent ideas that will fulfill their need to feel that the
> world as it exists makes sense. White people in the Delta re-
> sponded to their need to believe in the system of economic and
> political subjugation of blacks as just, fair, and inevitable by em-
> bracing the idea of black inferiority, and for them the primary ev-
> idence of this was lives like Ruby's.

These are startling ideas. They give Lemann's story altitude, a
liftoff from the tarmac of scenes and events to a vantage of meaning from the sky. But too much ozone can leave the reader feeling
oxygen deprived. Time to land. And so he does. Over the course
of the book, the movement Lemann creates, back and forth, back
and forth, between narrative and analysis, both instructs and delights the reader.

While this literary mix makes sense in nonfiction, you can
find analogies in great works of fiction going back to the earliest
expressions of English literature. The narrative line in Chaucer's
*Canterbury Tales* is a pilgrimage, but that story is interrupted by
the sacred and profane tales told by pilgrims. To many, *Moby
Dick* feels like two books: the tragic story of a crazed sea captain's
search for a deadly whale, interrupted time and again by explanations of whaling and the humdrum life of sailors. Even *Huckleberry Finn* describes a journey down a river, a narrative line with
several landings along the way.

Many newspapers and magazines have miniaturized this movement with a device called the *nut paragraph*. Any story that begins without the news requires a phrase, a sentence, a paragraph, a zone that answers the question "So what?" The nut paragraph answers that question for the reader. For more than thirty years, the *Wall Street Journal* has perfected this technique with whimsical front-page features. Reporter Ken Wells begins a story with an anecdote:

> Emma Thornton still shows up for work at 5 a.m. each day in her blue slacks, pinstripe shirt and rubber-soled shoes. A letter carrier for the U.S. Postal Service, she still dutifully sorts all the mail addressed to "One World Trade Center," and primes it for delivery.

But delivery to where and to whom? Why is this anecdote important? The answer requires a little altitude, a movement off the narrative line up to a higher level of meaning, a nut paragraph (in this case two paragraphs):

> Since Sept. 11, as many as 90,000 pieces of mail a day continue to flood in to the World Trade Center addresses that no longer exist and to thousands of people who aren't alive to receive them. On top of that is another mail surge set off by well-wishers from around the U.S. and the world — thousands of letters addressed to, among other salutations: "The People Hurt," "Any Police Department" and "The Working Dogs" of "Ground Zero, N.Y." Some of this mail contains money, food, even biscuits for the dogs that were used in the early days to help try to sniff out survivors.
>
> The mix of World Trade Center mail and Ground Zero mail represents a calamity for the U.S. Postal Service, which served 616 separate companies in the World Trade Center complex whose offices are now rubble or relocated.

No reader wants to be fooled by a story lead that promises narrative, only to discover a body dense with information. That is why the writer's movement from anecdote to meaning would be nothing more than a shell game without a return to the narrative line, to the world of letter carrier Emma Thornton. The writer delivers: "Her route in the North Tower has been transformed into a 6-by-6 steel cubicle . . . surrounded by tall metal racks of pigeonholes."

The broken line is a versatile story form. The writer can begin with narrative and move to explanation, or begin with straight information and then illustrate the facts with an anecdote. In either case, the easy swing, back and forth, can feel like clockwork.

## WORKSHOP

1. Read the work of Nicholas Lemann for examples of the broken line. Analyze his movement from narrative to analysis in books such as *The Promised Land: The Great Black Migration and How It Changed America* and *The Big Test: The Secret History of the American Meritocracy.*

2. Review your recent work. Find missed opportunities where you could have used the broken line.

3. Read the collection of *Wall Street Journal* features titled *Floating Off the Page.* Search it for interesting examples of the nut paragraph and the general movement between information and narrative.

4. As you review your work, look for examples where you have used the nut paragraph to reveal the higher meaning of the story. Pay attention to what comes after this paragraph. Do you move back to narrative, or are you practicing bait and switch on the reader?

5. As you read or write fiction, pay attention to the way information and explanation mix with narrative. Notice if facts are blended into the story or framed as separate elements.

# Tool 37

## In short works, don't waste a syllable.

*Shape short writing with wit and polish.*

I've seen the Hope Diamond at the Smithsonian. At forty-five carats, it is big and blue and buxom, but not beautiful. Smaller gems have more facets and reflect light with more brilliance. The same can be true of writing. In the ideal, the author of a great big novel should not waste a syllable, but he will, and chances are, in an ocean of words, the reader will not notice. The shorter the story form, the more precious is each word. So polish your jewelry.

Writing with video images and natural sound, Charles Kuralt mastered making each word — each pause — count:

> "I have fallen in love with American names," wrote the poet Stephen Vincent Benét.
>
> Well, really — how could you not? Not if you've been to Lick Skillet, Texas, and Bug Tussle, and Nip and Tuck, and Cut and Shoot. In California you can travel from Humbug Flat to Lousy Level, with a detour to Gouge Eye.
>
> Could the good people of Sleepy Eye, Minnesota, use some Hot Coffee, Mississippi, to wake them up?

You can go from Matrimony, North Carolina, to Caress, Virginia — or from Caress to Matrimony.

I have passed time in Monkey's Eyebrow, Kentucky, and Bowlegs and Tombstone, Big Chimney and Bull Town. And I liked Dwarf, Kentucky, though it's just a little town.

"I have fallen in love with American names." How could anybody not? (from *American Moments*)

Poet Peter Meinke taught me that short writing forms have three peculiar strengths: power, wit, and polish. Their brevity gives short works a focused power; it creates opportunity for wit; and it inspires the writer to polish, to reveal the luster of the language. Kuralt's essay exemplifies all three, capturing the power of the American language with witty examples off the American map, each clever name another facet cut into the diamond.

In his column for the *Charlotte Observer,* Jeff Elder wrote this response to a query about the extinction of an American species:

Passenger pigeons looked like mourning doves, but more colorful, with wine-red breasts, green necks and long blue tail feathers.

In 1800, there were 5 billion in North America. They were in such abundance that the new technology of the Industrial Revolution was enthusiastically employed to kill them. Telegraphs tracked their migration. Enormous roosts were gassed from trees while they slept. They were shipped to market in rail car after rail car after rail car. Farmers bought two dozen birds for a dollar, as hog feed.

In one human generation, America's most populous native bird was wiped out.

There's a stone wall in Wisconsin's Wyalusing State Park. On it is a bronze plaque of a bird. It reads: "This species became extinct through the avarice and thoughtlessness of man."

When I ask readers to appreciate this piece, they point to its many shiny facets. They notice:

- "The phrase 'rail car after rail car after rail car' looks like a rail car."
- "The words 'were gassed' carry connotations of a holocaust."
- "The first paragraph is filled with natural imagery, but the second contains the language of destructive technology."
- "Given their extinction, it is fitting that the pigeons looked like 'mourning' doves. The author takes advantage of that coincidence."

In short writing, the reader sees the ending from the get-go. With his ending, Elder adds a finish to the surface of the text.

Good fiction can be short or long, and longer works can contain powerful, witty, and polished shorter elements: anecdotes, scenes, descriptions, vignettes, set pieces that can be lifted out of the work for inspection and delight. Here is a paragraph from one of my favorite boyhood novels, *Herzog* by Saul Bellow:

> The wheels of the cars stormed underneath. Woods and pastures ran up and receded, the rails of sidings sheathed in rust, the dipping racing wires, and on the right the blue of the Sound, deeper, stronger than before. Then the enameled shells of the commuters' cars, and the heaped bodies of junk cars, the shapes of old New England mills with narrow, austere windows; villages, convents; tugboats moving in the swelling fabric-like water; and then plantations of pine, the needles on the ground of a life-giving russet color. So, thought Herzog, acknowledging that his imagination of the universe was elementary, the novae bursting and the worlds coming into being, the invisible magnetic spokes by means of which bodies kept one another in orbit. Astronomers made it all sound as though the gases were shaken up inside a flask. Then after many billions of years, light-years, this childlike but far from innocent creature, a straw hat on his head, and a heart in his

breast, part pure, part wicked, who would try to form his own shaky picture of this magnificent web.

It might take a long semester (and another book) to appreciate that passage. The wit — the governing intelligence — of the prose appears in those long fragments that capture the view from inside a moving train; in the exciting movement from junked cars to exploding stars; in that amazing image of human conflict and aspiration, topped off by a straw hat.

There is no more underdeveloped writing form in American journalism than the photo caption, but Jeffrey Page of the *Record* in New Jersey reveals the storytelling potential of this short form. Frank Sinatra had just died, so imagine a one-column photo that shows Sinatra from the waist up. He's wearing a tux with a black bow tie. He has a mike in his hand. He's crooning.

> If you saw a man in a tux and black bow tie swagger on stage like an elegant pirate, and if you had been told he would spend an hour singing Cole Porter, Gershwin and Rodgers and Hart, and if when he opened his mouth you heard a little of your life in his voice, and if you saw his body arch back on the high notes (the ones he insisted you hear and feel and live with him), and if his swing numbers made you want to bounce and be happy and be young and be carefree, and if when he sang "Try a Little Tenderness" and got to the line about a woman's wearing the same shabby dress it made you profoundly sad, and if years later you felt that his death made you a little less alive, you must have been watching this man who started as a saloon singer in Hoboken and went on to become the very definition of American popular music.

How did Page get away with a 166-word caption — written in a single sentence with the main clause near the end — without using the dead man's name? He tells me, "I know, I know, it violates every damned rule. Screw it. They keep telling us to take chances, right? So I did. . . . If you're a U.S. paper, and especially if you happen to be in New Jersey, you don't have to tell people that they're looking at a picture of Sinatra and not Mother Teresa."

## WORKSHOP

1. Reread the four short pieces above. Study them for their polished style. Make an inventory of the techniques the writers use to create their brilliant jewels.

2. Find the shortest piece you have written in the last year. Compare it to the examples in this section. Revise it so that every word works.

3. Write a photo caption like the one above. Practice, using news and feature photos from newspapers and magazines.

4. Begin a collection of short writing forms. Study how they are written. Make a list of techniques you could use in your writing.

# TOOL 38

◄○►

# Prefer archetypes to stereotypes.

*Use subtle symbols, not crashing cymbals.*

At some point, all writers confront the mythic, symbolic, and poetic, which is why they need to be aware (and beware) that common themes of narrative writing have deep roots in the culture of storytelling.

In 1971 John Pilger described a protest march by Vietnam veterans against the war:

> "The truth is out! Mickey Mouse is dead! The good guys are really the bad guys in disguise!" The speaker is William Wyman, from New York City. He is nineteen and has no legs. He sits in a wheelchair on the steps of the United States Congress, in the midst of a crowd of 300,000. . . . He has on green combat fatigues and the jacket is torn where he has ripped away the medals and the ribbons he has been given in exchange for his legs, and along with hundreds of other veterans, . . . he has hurled them on the Capitol steps and described them as shit; and now to those who form a ring of pity around him, he says, "Before I lost these legs, I killed and killed! We all did! Jesus, don't grieve for *me!*" (from *The Last Day*)

Since the Greek poet Homer sang *The Iliad* and *The Odyssey*, writers have composed stories of soldiers going off to war and their struggles to find a way home. This story pattern — often called *there and back* — is primeval and persistent, an archetype so deep within the culture of storytelling that we writers can succumb to its gravitational pull without even knowing it.

Ancient warriors fought for treasure and reputation, but in the passage above, the blessing becomes the curse. Symbols of bravery and duty turn to "shit" as angry veterans rip them from green jackets and toss them in protest. These soldiers return not to parades and glory, but to loss of faith, with limbs that can never be restored.

Good writers strive for originality, and they can achieve it by standing on a foundation of narrative archetypes, a set of story expectations that can be manipulated, frustrated, or fulfilled in novel ways, on behalf of the reader. Examples include:

the journey there and back
winning the prize
winning or losing the loved one
loss and restoration
the blessing becomes the curse
overcoming obstacles
the wasteland restored
rising from the ashes
the ugly duckling
the emperor has no clothes
descent into the underworld

My high school English teacher, Father Bernard Horst, taught me two important lessons about such archetypes. First, he said, if a wall appears in a story, chances are it's "more than just a wall." But, he was quick to add, when it comes to powerful writing, a symbol need not be a cymbal. Subtlety is a writer's virtue.

"The Dead," by Irish author James Joyce, is the tale of a married man named Gabriel who learns at a holiday party that his wife is haunted by the memory of a young man. Years earlier,

Michael Furey had died for her love. Countless times I have read the final paragraph:

> A few light taps upon the pane made him turn to the window. It had begun to snow again. He watched sleepily the flakes, silver and dark, falling obliquely against the lamplight. The time had come for him to set out on his journey westward. Yes, the newspapers were right: snow was general all over Ireland. It was falling on every part of the dark central plain, on the treeless hills, falling softly upon the Bog of Allen and farther westward, softly falling into the dark mutinous Shannon waves. It was falling, too, upon every part of the lonely churchyard on the hill where Michael Furey lay buried. It lay thickly drifted on the crooked crosses and headstones, on the spears of the little gate, on the barren thorns. His soul swooned slowly as he heard the snow falling faintly through the universe and faintly falling, like the descent of their last end, upon all the living and the dead.

When I first read that paragraph in college, it struck me with a force that transcended its literal meaning. It took me years to recognize the rich texture of its symbolic iconography: the names of the archangels Gabriel and Michael; the instruments of Christ's Passion ("crosses," "spears," and "thorns"); the evocation of the last days ("fall," "descent," "living and dead"). The fact that these were veiled from my first view is a virtue of the story, not a vice. It means that Joyce did not turn symbols into cymbals.

Some of the best writers in America work for National Public Radio. The stories they tell, making great use of natural sound, open a world to listeners, a world both fresh and distinctive, yet often informed by narrative archetypes. Margo Adler admitted as much when she revealed to me that her feature story on New York homeless people living in subway tunnels borrowed from her understanding of myths in which the hero descends into the underworld.

More recently, NPR reported the story of an autistic boy, Matt Savage, who had become, at age nine, an accomplished jazz musician. The reporter, Margo Melnicove, tapped into the standard form of the young hero who triumphs over obstacles. But the story gives us something more: "Until recently Matt Savage could not stand to hear music and most other sounds." Intensive auditory therapy turns the boy's neurological curse into a blessing, unleashing a passion for music expressed in jazz.

We use archetypes but should not let them use us. Consider as a cautionary tale, argues Tom French, the reporting on the dangers to women of silicone breast implants. Study after study confirms the medical safety of this procedure. Yet the culture refuses to accept it. Why? Perhaps it arises from the archetype that vanity should be punished, or that evil corporations are willing to profit from poisoning women's bodies.

Use archetypes. Don't let them use you.

## WORKSHOP

1. Read Joseph Campbell's *The Hero with a Thousand Faces* as an introduction to archetypal story forms.

2. As you read and hear coverage of military actions around the globe, look and listen for examples of the story forms described above.

3. Reexamine your writing from the last year. Can you identify pieces that fit or violate archetypal story patterns? Would you have written them differently?

4. Discuss Father Horst's advice: a symbol need not be a cymbal. Can you find a symbol in your work? Is it a cymbal?

## Tool 39

# Write toward an ending.

*Help readers close the circle of meaning.*

From our earliest years, we learn that stories have endings, however predictable. The prince and princess live happily ever after. The cowboy rides into the sunset. The witch is dead. The End. Or in the case of sci-fi movies: The End? Too often, in real life, the prince and princess get a divorce. The cowboy falls off his horse. The witch eats the baby. That's the dilemma for writers: reality is messy, but readers seek closure.

In 1999, the *New York Times* company commissioned me to write a newspaper serial novel I titled *Ain't Done Yet.* The story takes place in the months leading up to the millennium and involves an old investigative reporter tracking down the leader of a doomsday cult. I did not write from an outline, or even from much of a plan, but I knew that in the final chapter the good guy, who is afraid of heights and lightning, would be fighting the bad guy at midnight, atop a giant bridge, in a hurricane. In other words, I didn't know the stopping points along the way, but I wrote with an ending in mind. So I was not surprised to learn that J. K. Rowling began writing the Harry Potter series by crafting the final chapter of the last book and has even revealed the last word: "scar."

To write good endings you must read them, and few works of literature end with the poignant majesty of *The Great Gatsby*.

> And as I sat there brooding on the old, unknown world, I thought of Gatsby's wonder when he first picked out the green light at the end of Daisy's dock. He had come a long way to this blue lawn, and his dream must have seemed so close that he could hardly fail to grasp it. He did not know that it was already behind him, somewhere back in that vast obscurity beyond the city, where the dark fields of the republic rolled on under the night.

> Gatsby believed in the green light, the orgiastic future that year by year recedes before us. It eluded us then, but that's no matter — tomorrow we will run faster, stretch out our arms farther. . . . And one fine morning ——

> So we beat on, boats against the current, borne back ceaselessly into the past.

F. Scott Fitzgerald plants the seeds for this ending early in the novel, at the end of chapter one, when narrator Nick Carraway sees Gatsby for the first time:

> I decided to call to him. Miss Baker had mentioned him at dinner, and that would do for an introduction. But I didn't call to him, for he gave a sudden intimation that he was content to be alone — he stretched out his arms toward the dark water in a curious way, and, far as I was from him, I could have sworn he was trembling. Involuntarily I glanced seaward — and distinguished nothing except a single green light, minute and far away, that might have been the end of a dock. When I looked once more for Gatsby he had vanished, and I was alone again in the unquiet darkness.

Powerful lessons are embedded in this passage. Look at the phrase "unquiet darkness." The author shows us that sentences and paragraphs have endings too, even as those endings fore-shadow the book's final scene, some 160 pages later, when the green light, the dock, the outstretched arms will return, freighted with thematic significance.

These techniques are not for novelists alone. My colleague Chip Scanlan wrote an op-ed piece for the *New York Times* in which he argued that journalists should take lessons from citizens when it comes to asking good questions of politicians:

> As Bob Schieffer of CBS News polishes his questions for the final presidential debate tomorrow, he might want to take a page from Daniel Farley. And Randee Jacobs. And Norma-Jean Laurent, Mathew O'Brien, James Varner, Sarah Degenhart and Linda Grabel.

In that lead paragraph, Chip lists the names of citizens who had asked effective questions in the previous presidential debate. In his final paragraph, Chip closes the circle, replaying the chords he struck in the beginning:

> So tomorrow Mr. Schieffer can serve the public interest and teach his fellow reporters an important lesson about truth-gathering. He can model his questions on those asked by a handful of Missourians who understand the toughest questions are those that show the country what a candidate won't — or can't — answer.

There are endless ways to begin and end a piece of writing, but authors rely on a small toolbox of strategies, just as musicians do. In musical compositions, songs can build to a crescendo, or fade out, or stop short, or echo the opening. In written compositions, the author can choose from among these, and more:

• *Closing the circle.* The ending reminds us of the beginning by returning to an important place or by reintroducing us to a key character.

• *The tieback.* Humorist Dave Barry likes to tie his ending to some odd or offbeat element in the body of the story.

• *The time frame.* The writer creates a tick-tock structure, with time advancing relentlessly. To end the story, the writer decides what should happen last.

• *The space frame.* The writer is more concerned with place and geography than with time. The hurricane reporter moves us from location to location, revealing the terrible damage from the storm. To end, the writer selects our final destination.

• *The payoff.* The longer the story, the more important the payoff. This does not require a happy ending, but a satisfying one, a reward for a journey concluded, a secret revealed, a mystery solved.

• *The epilogue.* The story ends, but life goes on. How many times have you wondered, after the house lights come back on, what happened next to the characters in a movie? Readers come to care about characters in stories. An epilogue helps satisfy their curiosity.

• *Problem and solution.* This common structure suggests its own ending. The writer frames the problem at the top and then offers readers possible solutions and resolutions.

• *The apt quote.* Some characters speak in endings, capturing in their own words a neat summary or distillation of what has come before. In most cases, the writer can write it better than a character can say it. But not always.

• *Look to the future.* Most writing relates things that have happened in the past. But what do people say will happen next? What is the likely consequence of this decision or those events?

• *Mobilize the reader.* A good ending can point the reader in another direction. Attend this meeting. Read that book. Send an e-mail message to the senator. Donate blood for victims of a disaster.

You will write better endings if you remember that other parts of your story need endings too. Sentences have endings. Paragraphs have endings. As in *The Great Gatsby,* each of these mini-endings anticipates your finale.

I end with a warning. Avoid endings that go on and on like a Rachmaninoff concerto or a heavy metal ballad. Don't bury your ending. Put your hand over the last paragraph. Ask yourself, "What would happen if this ended here?" Move it up another paragraph and ask the same question until you find the natural stopping place.

## WORKSHOP

1. Review your most recent work. Place your hand over the last paragraph and ask yourself, "What would happen if my story ended here?" Is the natural ending hiding?

2. Read stories, listen to music, and watch movies with endings in mind. Pay close attention to details and themes planted early to bear fruit at the end.

3. Some journalists report for leads. Fewer report for endings. The next time you do research, watch and listen for a strong ending. What happens when you begin with an ending in mind?

4. Just for fun, take some of your recent work and switch the beginnings and the endings. Have you learned anything in the process?

—◄o►—

# Useful Habits

# Tool 40

◄◦►

# Draft a mission statement for your work.

*To sharpen your learning,*
*write about your writing.*

In 1996 the *St. Petersburg Times* published my series "Three Little Words," the story of a woman whose husband died of AIDS. The series ran for twenty-nine consecutive days and received unprecedented attention from local readers and journalists everywhere. A month of chapters was a lot to ask of readers. But here was the catch: no chapter contained more than 850 words, so you could keep up with the narrative by reading five minutes a day. Long series, short chapters.

Good writers turn stories into workshops, intense moments of learning in which they advance their craft. I learned more about reporting and telling stories from "Three Little Words" than from any other writing experience of my life. I'm still learning from it. But I did not learn how much I learned until I stumbled on a strategy I've turned into a tool: I write a mission statement for each story.

Whether we want them to or not, readers and critics examine the work of writers to grasp a sense of our mission and purpose. Too often, writers resist, as Mark Twain did when he posted this notice atop his most famous novel:

Persons attempting to find a motive in this narrative will be prosecuted; persons attempting to find a moral in it will be banished; persons attempting to find a plot in it will be shot.

But where the writer is silent, the critic, in this case Bernard De Voto, fills the void:

> *Huckleberry Finn* also has become a universal possession. It is a much deeper book than *Tom Sawyer* — deeper as of Mark Twain, of America, and of humanity. When after some stumbling it finds its purpose, it becomes an exploration of an entire society, the middle South along the river. In accomplishing this purpose it maintains at the level of genius Mark's judgment in full on the human race. It is well to remember that no one had spoken so witheringly to Americans about themselves before Huck raised his voice.

Most writers aspire to some invisible next step — for a story or a body of work. For some, this aspiration remains unfilled, becomes malignant, and metastasizes. Writing down your mission turns your vague hopes into language. By writing about your writing, you learn what you need to learn.

I scribbled my mission for "Three Little Words" on two pages of a legal pad. It covers the content and the form of the story, what I was writing about and how I wanted to write it. My mission begins: "I want to tell a human story, not just about AIDS, but of the deeply human themes of life, love, death, sorrow, hope, compassion, family, and community." The mission statement includes these goals:

• I want to portray my protagonist as a fully human character — and not some kind of cardboard saint.
• I want to do this so people can identify with and care for her and her family. It's so easy to see people with AIDS as "the other," the outcast, suffering sinners.

• I want to help illuminate AIDS, and help educate the public about key aspects of the disease.

• I want to advance the conversation about sexual culture and its impact on public health. I want to portray my protagonist's husband in a respectful way to avoid the common equation that Homosexuality = AIDS = Death.

• I want to do this in a form — twenty-nine short chapters — that will give people a chance to know, to learn, to care, and to hope.

As for the format:

• I want to restore the form of the serial narrative to newspapers — using the shortest chapters possible.

• I want to reconcile the values of short and long writing in American newspapers.

• I want to write each chapter with (a) a stand-alone quality, (b) a cliffhanger ending, (c) a sense of a new starting point.

I cannot overstate the value of this exercise. It gave me a view over the horizon as I drafted the story. This 250-word mission statement, which took about ten minutes to write, helped create a 25,000-word series. It provided the language I needed to share my hopes with other writers, editors, and readers. It could be tested, expanded, revised — and it was — during the writing process.

If you need encouragement to write a mission statement, let me assure you that many book authors write such expressions of purpose, which often show up as introductions or epilogues. Here's what Mark Bowden wrote at the conclusion of *Black Hawk Down,* a newspaper series, book, and movie about the American incursion into Somalia:

> When I began working on this project in 1996, my goal was simply to write a dramatic account of the battle. I had been struck by the intensity of the fight, and by the notion of ninety-nine Amer-

ican soldiers surrounded and trapped in an ancient African city fighting for their lives. My contribution would be to capture in words the experience of combat through the eyes and emotions of the soldiers involved, blending their urgent, human perspective with a military and political overview of their predicament.

As for the form of *Black Hawk Down*, Bowden wrote: "I wanted to combine the authority of a historical narrative with the emotion of the memoir, and write a story that read like fiction but was true."

Mission statements can bring into focus individual stories or an emerging body of work. For example,

- "I want to write a city government budget story so clear and interesting that it will attract readers who ignore such coverage."
- "I want to write a story about a World War II veteran but tell it from his point of view and in his voice."
- "I want to use crime stories in the newspaper to generate ideas for some fictional short stories."
- "I want to write unbiased stories on topics that polarize American citizens."

My "Three Little Words" workshop goes on and on as I hear from readers and journalists years later. From this distance, I see things I would have done differently: reduce the number of chapters; make the reporting and writing methods more transparent; create a straighter narrative line by eliminating one flashback. By writing that mission statement, I not only kick-started my own learning, but I also created a path where many others could ride along.

## WORKSHOP

1. Write a short mission statement for your next work. Use it to think about your writing strategies and aspirations. Share it

with someone else, as a reality check, and to get suggestions on how to achieve it.

2. Do the same for the body of your work. Where is the next level for you, that unseen but imagined destination over the horizon?

3. Study some of your old pieces, especially ones you deem successful. Write a mission statement after the fact, listing what you learned from each.

4. Imagine that famous authors had written mission statements for their masterpieces. What would they look like? Choose a favorite work and try to write one.

◄○►

# Turn procrastination into rehearsal.

*Plan and write it first in your head.*

Almost all writers procrastinate, so there's a good chance that you do too. Even among professionals, delay takes many forms. The film reviewer checks her e-mail messages for the tenth time. The novelist makes yet another trip to Starbucks, his fourth tall vanilla latte of the day. The famous scholar stares into space. So don't feel down if you find it hard to get started on that business report or college assignment.

The word *procrastinate* derives from the Latin word *cras,* meaning "tomorrow." Never write today what you can put off until tomorrow. With that sentiment, writers experience procrastination as a vice, not a virtue. During the process of not writing, we doubt ourselves and sacrifice the creative time we could use to build a draft.

What would happen if we viewed this period of delay not as something destructive, but as something constructive, even necessary? What if we found a new name for procrastination? What if we called it *rehearsal*?

A wonderful teacher of writing named Donald Graves began to notice that even little children engage in this process of mental preparation. He discovered that the best young writers rehearsed what they wanted to say. And why not? Don't teenagers rehearse a request for a later curfew, or an increase in allowance, or more time to complete a school assignment? We all rehearse, and that includes writers. Our problem is that we call it *procrastination* or *writer's block.*

Put simply, productive authors write stories in their heads. Blind poets and novelists such as Milton and Joyce did this, composing narrative passages through long nights only to be milked by transcribers in the morning. In this respect, the journalist is no different from the literary artist.

Put yourself in the place of a reporter covering a breaking news story, say a fire at a construction site. This reporter has spent a half day at the scene, filling a notebook with details. She must now drive twenty minutes to the newsroom. There the writer will have one hour before deadline. Adrenaline kicks in. No time to procrastinate. You must write today, not tomorrow.

Twenty minutes in the car are precious. Perhaps the reporter will turn off the radio and begin writing the story in her head. Some reporters can rehearse and remember several paragraphs. More likely, she may begin to imagine the three big parts of the story, or a few key expressions, or a focusing theme, perhaps a tentative lead: "High winds whipped a brush fire into an inferno Thursday, destroying most of a three-block condo complex on the outskirts of Ybor City."

Deadlines move writers to action, a reality that students in every discipline know too well. Exam writing is a form of writing on demand. Even when given two weeks to write a report, a typical student (I did it too!) waits until the last night to begin writing. The wise teacher confers with the student along the way to inspire research, preparation, and rehearsal. The wise student starts "writing" the paper the day it is assigned.

Foolish students wait too long to get their hands moving, until the pressures of deadline become irresistible and destructive. The alternative is to reframe the periods of inaction into forms of rehearsal. There is a Zen-like quality to such wisdom:

## WORKSHOP

1. For your next project, begin writing much earlier than you think you can. Write a summary of the day's research. Write a memo to yourself on what you've learned. Write a conditional first paragraph. Let all of this writing teach you what else you need to learn.

2. Have a conversation with a writer who seems to be procrastinating. In a diplomatic and supportive way, ask open-ended questions about the writing: What are you working on? How's it going? It turns out that talking about writing can transform procrastination into rehearsal, maybe even into action.

3. If you are a plodder, it may be worth your time to experiment with some forms of freewriting. If you are stuck, try writing on your current topic, for three minutes, as fast as you can. The purpose is not to create a draft, but to build momentum.

4. For one month, keep a daybook. Use it to jot down ideas and capture some phrases. Tell yourself that no sentence in your daybook will appear in your finished work. This will help lower your standards. Now write some memos to yourself. This early writing may help speed up your process.

# Tool 42

-◄◦►-

# Do your homework well in advance.

*Prepare yourself for the expected —*
*and unexpected.*

That great writing coach Prince Hamlet said it best: "the readiness is all." Good writers prepare for the next big writing project, even if it is not yet on the radar screen. They expect the unexpected. Like Batman, they cinch up a utility belt loaded with handy tools. They fill a reservoir of knowledge they can drain at a moment's notice.

Virginia Woolf argued famously that to prepare to write fiction, women would need some money and "a room of one's own." Her contemporary, Dorothea Brande, described a more disciplined form of writing preparation:

> Mind you, you are not yet to write it. The work you are doing on it is preliminary. For a day or two you are going to immerse yourself in these details; you are going to think about them consciously, turning if necessary to books of reference to fill in your facts. Then you are going to dream about it. . . . There will seem no end to the stuff that you can find to work over. What does the heroine look like? Was she an only child, or the eldest of several? How was she educated? Does she work? (from *Becoming a Writer*)

Control of a nation, victory in the nuclear age, strategic domination of the globe.

The titans of Nixon's age gathered again today, on an unseasonably cold and gray afternoon, and now they were white-haired or balding, their steel was rusting, their skin had begun to sag, their eyesight was failing. They were invited to contemplate where power leads.

Such work is no accident, and Von Drehle shares the secrets of readiness. Under pressure, he falls back on the basics, thinks about what happened, why it matters, and how he can turn it into a story. He must do enough homework to answer these three questions:

1. What's the point?
2. Why is this story being told?
3. What does it say about life, about the world, about the times we live in?

I end with the story of a famous foreign correspondent and novelist, Laurence Stallings, who was assigned in 1925 to cover a big college football game between Pennsylvania and Illinois. The star of the day was Red Grange. Known as the Galloping Ghost, Grange dazzled the crowd with 363 yards of total offense, leading the Illini to a 24–2 upset victory over Penn.

The famous journalist and author was awestruck. Red Smith wrote that Stallings "clutched at his haircut" as he paced up and down the pressbox. How could anyone cover this event? "It's too big," he said, "I can't write it," this coming from a man who had once covered World War I.

Someone should have quoted Shakespeare to him: "the readiness is all."

## WORKSHOP

1. With the help of a friend, list possible big writing projects that could emerge from your specialty or area of interest. Begin homework on these topics, preparation that will help you down the road.

2. As you watch big sporting events, such as the World Series or the Super Bowl or the Olympics, rehearse in your head possible scenes you would write for the most dramatic stories. Compare and contrast your approaches with those that appear in print and on air.

3. Big stories need good titles. Review your recent work to see if your titles match the intensity and quality of the text. For your next project, brainstorm titles early in the process to focus your research and writing.

4. If you write fiction, review the process of research and preparation for novelists described by Brande and Ford. Try using those strategies as homework for a short story. If they work for you, apply them to more ambitious projects.

stories is to use their X-ray vision. (After all, Superman was also a newspaper writer, and boy, could he type fast.) X-ray reading helps you see through the text of the story. Beneath the surface grinds the invisible machinery of grammar, language, syntax, and rhetoric, the gears of making meaning, the hardware of the trade.

Here are some reading tricks for writers:

- Read to listen to the voice of the writer.
- Read the newspaper in search of underdeveloped story ideas.
- Read online to experience a variety of new storytelling forms.
- Read entire books when they compel you; but also taste bits of books.
- In choosing what to read, be directed less by the advice of others and more by your writing compass.
- Sample — for free — a wide selection of current magazines and journals in bookstores that serve coffee.
- Read on topics outside your discipline, such as architecture, astronomy, economics, and photography.
- Read with a pen nearby. Write in the margins. Talk back to the author. Mark interesting passages. Ask questions of the text.

I temper my enthusiasm for reading with this caution: there will be times in the middle of a writing project when you may want to stop reading. While drafting the tools in this book, I stopped reading about writing. I did not want my fascination with the topic to seduce me away from my writing time; nor did I want to be unduly influenced by the ideas of others; nor did I wish to be discouraged by the brilliance of finished, published work.

Scholars argue that reading is a triangular transaction — a ménage à trois — among author, text, and reader. The author may create the text, argues Louise Rosenblatt, but the reader turns it into a story. So the reader is a writer after all. Voilà!

WORKSHOP

1. Go to a bookstore and immerse yourself in the magazine section. Drink as much coffee as you need. Look for publications that stretch your interest and challenge your standards.

2. Find an author to admire. Read several works by this writer with a pen in hand. Mark passages that work in special ways. Show these to a friend and X-ray them together. What writing tools did you find?

3. Read an interesting passage aloud. Then put it away and freewrite on a topic of your choice. Explore the influence that flows from this experiment.

4. If you are an editor or a teacher, use a shared reading experience to inspire your writers or students. Or do this with a friend. Swap stories you like and X-ray them. Why do they work? What tools of language do they reveal?

# Save string.

*For big projects, save scraps others would toss.*

When writers tell me stories about working on big projects, they use one of two metaphors to describe their method. The first is *composting*. To grow a good garden, you need to fertilize the soil. So some gardeners build compost heaps in their yards, mounds of organic material containing scraps, like banana peels, that others would throw away. The second is *saving string*. Bits of twine get rolled into tiny balls that grow into bigger balls that grow, in extreme cases, into balls of civic pride. A man named Francis Johnson created a ball of twine that weighed more than 17,000 pounds, was twelve feet in diameter, and became the main roadside attraction for the town of Darwin, Minnesota.

Johnson should become patron saint of those who save bits of writing, hoping that one day they will grow into something publishable. Here's how it works for me: I will be struck by a theme or issue in politics or culture. Right now, for example, I am fascinated by the plight of boys. As the father of three daughters, I've watched many young women succeed in education and flourish in careers, while young men lag behind. I lack the time or knowledge to write about this topic now, but maybe I will someday. My chances will improve if I begin to save string.

To save string, I need a simple file box. I prefer the plastic ones that look like milk crates. I display the box in my office and put a label on it, say, "The Plight of Boys." As soon as I declare my interest in an important topic, a number of things happen. I notice more things about my topic. Then I have conversations about it with friends and colleagues. They feed my interest. One by one, my box fills with items: an analysis of graduation rates of boys versus girls; a feature on whether video games help or hinder the development of boys; a story about decreasing participation by boys in high school sports. This is a big topic, so I take my time. Weeks and weeks pass, sometimes months and months, and one day I'll look over at my box and hear it whisper, "It's time." I'm amazed at its fullness, and even more astonished at how much I've learned just by saving string.

For me this process also works for fiction. During a long plane trip, I scribbled the opening scenes of a short novel titled *Trash Baby*, in which a thirteen-year-old boy finds a baby abandoned near a Dumpster. As the story took shape over months, I saved more and more string: newspaper stories about abandoned babies, manslaughter trials of distraught mothers, the development of "safe haven" laws to allow mothers to drop off newborns at hospitals with no questions asked.

Book authors testify to a single-minded immersion in a subject or character, a habit that can lead to the obsessive saving of string. Biographer David McCullough described in the *Washington Post* the depths of his passion:

> For about 6 years now, in the time it's taken to write my biography of John Adams, I have largely abandoned reading anything written in our own day. For along with research of the kind to be expected with such a book, I have been trying as much as possible to know Adams through what he read as well as what he wrote, and the result has been one of the most enjoyable forays of my writing life.

Once the writer builds a compost mountain, what happens next? Former secretary of state and author George P. Shultz explained to the *Post* how he dug in to write a book:

> I spread out voluminous material on the large conference-room table where I worked. As I read through what I had at hand for a particular chapter, I took time to think about it. After I inhaled the material and searched out still more, sometimes from the public record, sometimes from my assistant's notes and my other archival sources, I made an outline and then started writing. I could see how the writing forced me to be more rigorous, to rethink, to look up new information, to check facts meticulously, to recognize where a piece was missing, here and there, and where the logic was flawed.

I identify with this method: save string, gather piles of research, be attentive to when it's time to write, write earlier than you think you can, let those early drafts drive you to additional research and organization.

This process may appear too long and unproductive, with too much saving, storing, and thinking. The trick for me is to grow several crops at the same time. Fertilize one crop, even as you harvest another. In my office I have several boxes with labels on them:

- I have an AIDS box, which culminated in the publication of the series "Three Little Words."
- I have a millennium box, which culminated in publication of the serialized newspaper novel *Ain't Done Yet.*
- I have a Holocaust and anti-Semitism box, which culminated in the series "Sadie's Ring." It is now a book manuscript looking for a home.
- I have a box titled "Civil Rights," which culminated in an anthology of newspaper columns from the 1960s on racial justice in the South.

- I have a box titled "Formative Reading," bursting with materials on critical literacy, which I thought would become a book. It has produced several articles.
- I have a box called "World War II," which produced two newspaper features, one of which might become a small book someday.

Inventory the topics in my boxes: AIDS, the Holocaust, racial justice, the millennium, World War II, literacy. These are topics of inexhaustible interest, capable of generating a lifetime of reporting, storytelling, and analysis. Each one, in fact, is so huge, so imposing, it threatens to overpower the writer's energy and imagination. This is the reason to save string. Item by item, anecdote by anecdote, statistic by statistic, your boxes of curiosity fill up without effort, creating a literary life cycle: planting, cultivation, and harvesting.

Right now, buried in routine, you feel you lack the time and energy to undertake enterprising work. Maybe you have a day job but want to research a novel. Perhaps you feel worn out writing many short items every day for a company newsletter. Where will you find the energy to write in depth? If you rebel against the clutter of paper piled in a box, start an electronic file or a paper file in a manila folder. As you perform your routine work, talk about your special interest. Gather opinions and anecdotes from across the landscape. Scribble them down, one by one, fragment by fragment, until one day you look up and see a monument of persistence, ready to be mounted in the town square.

## WORKSHOP

1. Review your writing from the last couple of years. List your big categories of interest and curiosity. For which of those topics do you want to save string?

2. What other big topics not reflected in your current writing interest you? Which one fascinates you the most? Create a box or a file and label it.

3. Do an Internet search on one of your new topics. Spend time exploring. Add to your file some items from blogs and Web sites that connect with your interest.

4. Imagine you are writing a work of fiction on a theme of passionate interest. Brainstorm the methods you could use to gather string on your topic.

# TOOL 45

-◄o►-

## Break long projects into parts.

*Then assemble the pieces into something whole.*

Anne Lamott's book *Bird by Bird* gets its title from an anecdote about her brother. At the age of ten, he struggled with a school report on birds. Lamott describes him as "immobilized by the hugeness of the task ahead," but then, "my father sat down beside him, put his arm around my brother's shoulder, and said, 'Bird by bird, buddy. Just take it bird by bird.' "

We all need such coaching to remind us to break long projects into parts, long stories into chapters, long chapters into episodes. Such advice is both encouraging and practical.

Where writers gather, I often ask this question: "How many of you have run a marathon?" In a group of one hundred, maybe one or two will raise a hand. "If properly trained and motivated, how many of you think you could run twenty-six miles?" A half dozen more. "What if I gave you fifty-two days to do it, so you only had to run a half mile a day?" Most of the hands in the room go up.

Most doctoral students who finish all their class work, and pass all examinations, and complete research for a dissertation never get a Ph.D. Why? Because they lack the simple discipline required to finish the writing. If they sat each morning for an hour to write a single page — 250 words — they could finish a thesis in less than a year.

When my children were young, I volunteered to teach writing in their elementary school. After each class, I scribbled notes in a journal, never taking more than ten minutes to complete the task. What had I learned that day? How did the children respond? Why was that bright student staring into space? After three years, I thought I might have a book in me about teaching children to write. I had never written a book and did not know how to begin, so I transcribed my journal entries. The result was about 250 pages of typed text, not yet a book, but a sturdy foundation for what was to become *Free to Write: A Journalist Teaches Young Writers.*

Tiny drops of writing become puddles that become rivulets that become streams that become deep ponds.

The power of this writing habit is overwhelming, like Harry Potter being told for the first time that he is a famous wizard. You are now reading Tool 45 — in what was once a yearlong online series — headed for Tool 50. If I had said to my editors, "You know, I'd like to write a book of writing tools," I never would have done the work. At the front end, book projects seem impossible to get your arms around, like hugging a polar bear. Instead, I pitched the writing tools project as fifty short essays, delivered at the rate of one or two per week.

The same strategy could have produced the book on my nightstand, *The Lord Is My Shepherd* by Harold Kushner, a superb writer and teacher. The foreword begins:

> I have been thinking about the ideas in this book for more than forty years, since I was first ordained as a rabbi. Every time I would read the Twenty-third Psalm at a funeral or memorial service, or at the bedside of an ailing congregant, I would be struck by its power to comfort the grieving and calm the fearful. The real impetus for this book came in the wake of the terrible events of September 11, 2001. In the days following the attacks, people on the street and television interviewers would ask me, "Where was

God? How could God let this happen?" I found myself responding, "God's promise was never that life would be fair. God's promise was that, when we had to confront the unfairness of life, we would not have to do it alone for He would be with us." And I realized I had found that answer in the Twenty-third Psalm.

Writers search for the focus of a story, and what a strong focusing idea to write a book about a single fourteen-line prayer, one that has such significance within the Judeo-Christian context. Imagine writing a book about the Lord's Prayer, or the Ave Maria, or one of Shakespeare's sonnets. But how to organize the writing and reading of such a book? Kushner provides an elegant solution: each chapter is devoted to one line of the psalm. So there is a chapter called "The Lord Is My Shepherd," and another called "Though I Walk through the Valley of the Shadow of Death," and another called "My Cup Runneth Over." A 175-page national bestseller is divided into an introduction and fourteen short chapters, handy units for the writer and the reader.

Bird by bird, tool by tool, line by line.

### WORKSHOP

1. Admit it. You want to write something bigger than you've ever written before, but you can't get your arms around the project. The length or breadth of it intimidates you. Cut up the monster. In a daybook or journal, break it up into its smallest parts: chapters, sections, episodes, vignettes. Without referring to any notes or research materials, write one of these small units. See what happens.

2. The next time you are in a bookstore, take a peek at several big volumes: novels, memoirs, almanacs. Check out the table of contents and figure out the structural units that make up the book. Now check individual chapters to see how they subdivide. Notice these small parts in the rest of your reading.

3. Traditionally, the Bible comprises books, chapters, and verses. Browse through the King James Version and pay attention

to how the books divide. Notice the differences, for example, among Genesis, Psalms, and the Song of Songs.

4. Before you draft your next story, scribble on a legal pad what you conceive as the parts of the story. Don't just write down beginning, middle, and end. Try writing down the smaller parts of those bigger parts.

## TOOL 46

—◄○►—

# Take an interest in all crafts
# that support your work.

*To do your best, help others do their best.*

I abhor the image of the writer as a solitary figure. That romantic stereotype, associated with loneliness and struggle, has alienated many aspiring writers and blown a cloud over one of the craft's shining truths: that writing is a social activity.

I remember my first published work, a Christmas poem for a 1958 school newspaper:

> On a cold and snowy night
> In a land so far away,
> A babe was born in Bethlehem,
> Born on Christmas Day.
> They laid Him in a manger,
> No place for a king,
> But it seemed just like a palace
> When they heard the angels sing.

I was a proud ten-year-old poet when I saw my name emblazoned above the text, but it took a small Long Island village to publish that singsongy verse. It took a teacher to invite us to write. It took my mother to brainstorm with me. It took another student to draw a little illustration. It took a school clerk to type stories onto mimeographs and another to run them off and distribute them. It took the students and some of their parents to praise me. With that early experience shaping my writer's soul, I ask forgiveness for my visceral rejection of the tormented writer on the mountaintop.

If you aspire to improve as a writer, begin with your self-interest: if your story is well edited, accompanied by a powerful photograph, on a page that is well designed, it will look more important and more people will read it. You would be foolish to ignore or belittle that power.

In fact, you will never reach your potential as a writer unless you take an interest in all of the associated literary crafts. Cultivate this habit: ask questions about the crafts of copyediting, photography, illustration, graphics, design, and Web site production. You need not become an expert in these fields, but it's your duty to be curious and engaged. One day, you will talk about these crafts without an accent.

Just as important, make nice with people who come forth to help you. If you do not yet write for publication or as part of your job, practice collaboration with the people who help you now: friends, teachers, fellow students, members of a writing group or book club, fellow bloggers or Web site editors and designers.

To find the right mood, imagine that you are the author of a wonderful novel that has been optioned to a film studio. You have received a huge advance to write the screenplay. Now think of all the associated crafts that will contribute to the perfection of your work. Think about the directors and actors, the cinematographer, the film editor, the set designer, the score composer, and many more. Carry the vision of that rich collaboration into all of your writing.

As I develop as an author and journalist, these key figures continue to make my work better:

• *Copyeditors.* Ignore the traditional antagonism that leads writers to believe that copyeditors are vampires who work at night and suck the life out of stories. Instead, think of copyeditors as champions of standards, invaluable test readers, your last line of defense. I once wrote a story about two brothers with terrible physical handicaps, boys who had been separated for years. I described their wonderful reunion, how the brothers watched cartoons and fed each other Fruit Loops. A copyeditor, Ed Merrick, called me to check on the story. He offered his praise for a job well done, but said he had sent a news clerk down to the supermarket (this was before the convenience of the Internet) to check on the spelling of *Fruit Loops.* Sure enough, the correct spelling was *Froot Loops.* Nice catch. The last thing I wanted was for the reader to notice this mistake, especially at a high point in the story. Years later, I would see Ed and give him the thumbs-up sign in gratitude for his Froot Loops fix. Talk to copyeditors. Learn their names. Embrace them as fellow writers and lovers of language. Feed them chocolate.

• *Photographers.* Make sure photo assignments are considered early in the process, not as an afterthought. Using television journalism as a model, look for opportunities for you and the photographer to work side by side. Help the photographer understand your vision of the work. Ask questions about what the photographer sees. Use the work of the photographer to document the story. Let the photographer teach you about focus, framing, composition, and lighting. Ask the photographer what you can do to help.

• *Designers.* As your project develops, make sure you include visual artists in the conversation early in the process. Learn from them what you need to see and bring back from a scene, material that can be converted into sparkling visual and design elements. Ask your editor and visual journalists how you can help them while you are doing research or writing early drafts.

Remember that good work takes time — and not just for you. Learn to meet your deadlines to give others time to do their jobs. Even if you lack the authority to convene conversations, encourage early planning that includes all key players. The more interested you become in the associated crafts, the more you will be invited into decisions about how your work is presented and perceived.

Between 2001 and 2005, I wrote more than five hundred columns and essays for the Poynter Institute Web site. I am no expert on how to produce a story across media platforms. But I am adapting my writing tools and habits to a brave new world of media technology. The opportunity to write in different voices, the chance to interact with the audience, the adventure of crossing old boundaries — all these require a richer imagination and greater collaboration than ever before.

If you work hard at your cross-disciplinary education, supporting the marriage of words and visuals, you will prepare yourself for a future of innovation and creativity. You can do this without sacrificing the enduring values of your craft. This requires not just the Golden Rule — treat others the way *you* want to be treated — but what my old colleague Bill Boyd calls the Platinum Rule: Treat others the way *they* want to be treated. How does the copyeditor want to be treated? What does the photographer need to do her best work? And what gives the designer satisfaction? The only way to know for sure is to ask.

## WORKSHOP

1. If you work in a news organization or for a publishing house, if you are writing a film documentary or a nonfiction narrative, if you write for a Web site or a newsletter, you depend on others to accomplish your best work. List the names of these people. Make sure you have their phone numbers and e-mail addresses.

2. Develop a schedule of conversations with each person on your list. Apply the Platinum Rule. Ask them what they need to do their best work.

3. Encourage the kind of support you desire. Don't just com-

plain. If someone has written a good headline or saved you from a mistake, reward that good work with praise.

4. Read about the associated crafts. Find a good book on photography. Read some design magazines. Listen to conversations about these crafts and develop a lexicon so that you can chime in.

―◄◦►―

# Recruit your own support group.

*Create a corps of helpers for feedback.*

Now that we have dismantled the disabling myth of authorship as a lonely craft, you can free yourself of the need to rent a loft overlooking the ocean, your only companions a portable typewriter, a bottle of gin, and a kitty named Hemingway.

In the real world, writing is more like line dancing, a social function with many partners. As we've seen, some of those partners — a writing teacher, a workshop group, a Web producer, a copyeditor — may be assigned to us. Other helpers can and should be of our choosing.

You must create a system of support both wide and deep. If you limit yourself to one classroom teacher or one editor, you will not get the help you need. You must create a network of friends, colleagues, editors, and coaches who can offer feedback — and maybe an occasional feedbag.

My support system changes as I change. I'm a different writer and person than I was twenty years ago, so I refresh the team I have assigned to help me. This should be a radical concept to you, especially if you are starting out as a writer. You may say to yourself, I'd be happy with any feedback at all. I am saying to you, don't settle for what is given to you. Whatever it is, it is not enough. Work on developing the support system you need and deserve.

Here are the kinds of people I need:

• *A helper who keeps me going.* For years, my teaching partner Chip Scanlan has played this role for me, especially when I am working on a long project. Chip has a rare quality as a colleague: he is capable of withholding negative judgments. He says to me, over and over again, "Keep going. Keep writing. We'll talk about that later."

• *A helper who understands my idiosyncrasies.* All writers have quirks. The fleas come with the dog. I find it almost unbearable to read my published work in the newspaper. I assume I'll encounter some terrible mistake. My wife, Karen, understands this. While I cower under the covers with my dog, Rex, she sits at the breakfast table, crunching her Rice Chex, reading my story in the paper and making sure no unforeseen horror has appeared. "All clear," she says, to my relief.

• *A helper willing to answer my questions.* For many years writing coach Donald Murray has been willing to read my drafts, and he begins by asking me what I need from him. In other words, "How would you like me to read this?" or "What kind of reading are you looking for?" My response might be, "Is this too Catholic?" or "Does this seem real enough to publish as a memoir?" or "Just let me know if you find this interesting." Murray is always generous, but it helps us both when he reads with a focus in mind.

• *An expert helper to match my topic.* My current interest often dictates the kind of helper I need. When I wrote about the Holocaust and the history of anti-Semitism, I depended on the wisdom and experience of a rabbi, Haim Horowitz. When I wrote about AIDS, I turned to an oncologist, Dr. Jeffrey Paonessa. Such people may begin as interview subjects, but the deeper you get into a topic, the more they can turn into sounding boards and confidants.

• *A helper who runs interference.* On fire with enthusiasm for one writing project, I'd wake up early, get into the office before daylight, and try to write for a couple of hours before my other work responsibilities forced an interruption. Joyce Barrett blessed me with her assistance for twenty years. I especially remember the morning she came to work, saw that I was writing, closed my office door, and put a motel-style Do Not Disturb sign on the handle. That's good downfield blocking.

• *A coach who helps me figure out what works and what needs work.* For more than a year, an intern named Ellen Sung edited a column I wrote for the Poynter Web site. In most ways, the two of us could not have been more different. I was older, white, male, with a print orientation. Ellen was twenty-four years old, Chinese American, female, and thrived online. She was well read, curious, with mature sensibilities as an editor. She could articulate the strengths of a column, asked great questions that would lead to revisions and clarifications, and framed negative criticism with persuasive diplomacy. Ellen now works as a newspaper reporter, but she still belongs to my network, willing to help at a moment's notice.

You may choose these helpers one by one, but over time they form a network, with you at the center. You may address them as a group via e-mail or ask them in various combinations to help you solve a problem. You can test the criticism of one against the wisdom of another. You can fire one who gets too bossy. You can send another flowers or a bottle of wine. It's good, on occasion, for the writer to be the king — or queen.

## WORKSHOP

1. Look at the six categories of helpers described above. Make a list of six people who might be able to serve you in these capacities. Rehearse a conversation with each with the goal of expanding your network.

2. Make a list of the specific ways an editor, teacher, or friend

has helped you improve a story. Have you approached that person to express thanks for such help? If not, go out of your way the next time it happens.

3. Admit it. An editor or teacher is driving you crazy. Rehearse a conversation in which you describe the behavior that hinders your work. Can you find a way to communicate this with civility and diplomacy? "Jim, the last few times I've suggested a story idea to you, you've rejected it. I find this discouraging. I'd like to work on some of these stories. Is this something we can talk about?"

4. Make a list of the members of your writing posse. Next to their names, list the roles they play for you. Who else do you need to accomplish your best work?

—◄○►—

# Limit self-criticism in early drafts.

*Turn it loose during revision.*

As I peruse my collection of books on writing, I find they fall into two broad categories. In one box, I find books such as *The Elements of Style* and *On Writing Well*. These classics by Strunk and White and William Zinsser capture writing as a craft, so they concern themselves with toolboxes and blueprints. In the other box, I find works such as *Bird by Bird* and *Wild Mind*. In these works by Anne Lamott and Natalie Goldberg, I'm less likely to find advice on technique than on living a life of language, of seeing a world of stories.

The standards for this second category go back at least to the 1930s when Dorothea Brande wrote *Becoming a Writer* (1934) and Brenda Ueland wrote *If You Want to Write* (1938). It is a blessing that both books remain in print, inviting a new generation into the community of writers.

Brande expresses her preference for coffee, a medium-soft lead pencil, and a noiseless portable typewriter. She offers advice on what writers should read and when they should write. Her concerns include meditation, imitation, practice, and recreation. But she is most powerful on the topic of self-criticism. To become a fluent writer, she argues, one must silence the internal critic early in the process. The critic becomes useful only when enough work has been done to warrant evaluation and revision. Influenced by Freud, Brande argues that during the early stages of creation, the writer should write freely, "harnessing the unconscious":

> Up to this point it is best to resist the temptation to reread your productions. While you are training yourself into facility in writing and teaching yourself to start writing whenever and wherever opportunity offers, the less you turn a critical eye upon your own material the better — even for a cursory survey. The excellence or triteness of your writing was not the matter under consideration. But now, turning back to see what it may reveal under a dispassionate survey, you may find those outpourings very enlightening.

Four decades later, another writer, Gail Godwin, would cover the same territory in an essay titled "The Watcher at the Gate." For Godwin, the Watcher is the "restraining critic who lived inside me," and who appeared in many forms to lock the doors of her creativity.

> It is amazing the lengths a Watcher will go to keep you from pursuing the flow of your imagination. Watchers are notorious pencil sharpeners, ribbon changers, plant waterers, home repairers and abhorrers of messy rooms or messy pages. They are compulsive looker-uppers. They cultivate self-important eccentricities they think are suitable for "writers." And they'd rather die (and kill your inspiration with them) than risk making a fool of themselves.

Like Brande, Godwin draws her central images from Freud, who quotes Friedrich von Schiller: "In the case of a creative mind . . . the intellect has withdrawn its watchers from the gates, and the ideas rush in . . . and only then does it review and inspect the multitude." Schiller chides a friend: "You reject too soon and discriminate too severely."

Brenda Ueland fights the battle against internal and external criticism with the passion of a warrior princess and the zeal of a suffragette. She titles one chapter, "Why women who do too much housework should neglect it for their writing." In another chapter, she argues, "Everybody is talented, original and has something important to say."

She notes that "all people who try to write . . . become anxious, timid, contracted, become perfectionists, so terribly afraid that they may put something down that is not as good as Shakespeare." That is one loud critical voice, one bug-eyed watcher.

> And so no wonder you don't write and put it off month after month, decade after decade. For when you write, if it is to be any good at all, you must feel free, — free and not anxious. The only good teachers for you are those friends who love you, who think you are interesting, or very important, or wonderfully funny; whose attitude is:

> "Tell me more. Tell me all you can. I want to understand more about everything you feel and know and all the changes inside and out of you. Let more come out."

> And if you have no such friend, — and you want to write, — well then you must imagine one.

For Godwin, weapons against the Watcher include such things as deadlines, writing fast, writing at odd times, writing when you're tired, writing on cheap paper, writing in surprising forms from which no one expects excellence.

So far, I have emphasized only one side of the equation: the value of silencing the voice of the internal critic early in the process. You have a right to ask, "But when the Voice speaks out during revision, what should I hope she says to me?" The Voice will be a more useful critic, I say immodestly, after exposure to this set of tools. Armed with tools, the Voice might say, "Do you need that adverb?" Or, "Is this the place for a gold coin?" Or, "Isn't it time for you to climb down the ladder of abstraction and offer a good example?"

The important lesson is this: the self-conscious application of all writing advice will turn you to stone if you try to do it too early, or if you misapply it as orthodoxy. Dorothea Brande, Brenda Ueland, Gail Godwin — these writers have the right idea. There's enough hard critical work to do and enough criticism to face. So begin with a gift to yourself, maybe that first cup of coffee.

## WORKSHOP

1. Be more conscious of those moments when the critical voice shouts or whispers in your ear. What is the Voice saying? Make a list of the negative things the Voice is likely to say about you. Now burn the list and flush the ashes.

2. Have at least one person in your circle of helpers who praises you without reservation, who is willing to tell you what works in your story, even when you know that much work remains to be done. Can you play this role in the life of another writer?

3. Be aware of the moment in the writing process when you are ready to call the critical voice onstage. Make a list of the kinds of questions you'd like the Voice to ask you. Consult these writing tools to form the list.

4. Godwin writes that she fools the Watcher by disguising the form of the writing. So if she is working on a draft of a short story, she may disguise it in the form of a letter. The next time you struggle with a story, put a salutation at the top ("Dear Friend") and write a message to your friend about the story. See what happens.

—◄◦►—

# Learn from your critics.

*Tolerate even unreasonable criticism.*

I've saved one of the hardest lessons for near the end. I don't know anyone who enjoys negative criticism, especially of creative work. But such criticism can be priceless if you learn how to use it. The right frame of mind can transform criticism that is nasty, petty, insincere, biased, and even profane, into gold.

This alchemy requires one magic strategy: the receptive writer must convert debate into conversation. In a debate, one side listens only to find a counterargument. In a conversation, there is give and take. A debate ends with a winner and a loser. A conversation can conclude with both sides learning, and a promise of more good talk to come.

I long ago made a resolution that will sound like an impossible task: I never defend my work against criticism.

Not defend your work? That sounds as reasonable as not blowing out a match as it burns toward your fingers. The reflex to defend your work is a force of nature, the literary equivalent of fight or flight.

Let me offer a hypothetical example. Let's say I've written this news lead out of a city council meeting: "Should the Seattle police be able to peep at the peepers in the peep shows?" Now say I receive this criticism from an editor or teacher: "Roy, you've got much too much peeping going on here for my taste. You've turned a serious story about privacy into a cute play on words. I was expecting Little Bo Peep to show up any minute. Ha, ha, ha."

Such criticism is likely to make me angry and defensive, but I've come to believe that argument is useless. I like all that peeping. My critic hates it. He prefers a lead such as "The city council debated whether the Seattle police should be able to go undercover as part of the effort to see whether adult businesses are adhering to municipal regulations of their activities." My critic suffers from omnivorous solemnity. He thinks I suffer from irreversible levity.

One of the oldest bits of wisdom about art goes like this, and please excuse the Latin: "De gustibus non est disputandum." There can be no arguing about matters of taste. I think *Moby Dick* is too long. You think abstract art is too abstract. My chili is too spicy. You reach for the Tabasco.

What, then, is the alternative to a donnybrook? If I don't fight to defend my work, won't I lose control to people who don't share my values?

Here's the alternative: never defend your work; instead, explain what you were trying to accomplish. So: "Jack, I can see that all that peeping in my lead didn't work for you. I was just trying to find a way for readers to be able to see the impact of this policy. I didn't want to let the police action get lost in a lot of bureaucratic language." Such a response is more likely to turn a debate (which the writer will lose) into a conversation (in which the critic might convert from adversary to ally).

My friend Anthea Penrose issued a criticism of the short chapters of my serial narrative "Three Little Words." She said something like, "It wasn't enough for me. Just when I was getting into it, you were finished. I wanted more."

How could I possibly change her mind? And why should I? If the chapters are too short for her, they are too short. So here is my response: "Anthea, you're not the first one to respond that way to the short chapters. They do not work for some readers. By using short chapters, I was trying to lure time-starved readers who say they never read long, enterprising work. I've received a few messages from readers who told me they appreciate my concern for their time, that this is the first series in a newspaper that they have ever read."

Another critic: "I hated the way you ended that chapter after Jane was tested for HIV and didn't tell me the results of the test right away. I wanted to know *now*. But you made me wait until the next day's paper. I thought that was really exploitative."

My response: "You know, Jane was tested a number of times, and back then she might have had to wait a couple of weeks for the results. I came to understand how excruciating it must have been to wait that long, with life and death in the balance. So I thought if I made the reader wait overnight for the results, it would get you to better understand her plight."

Such a response always softened the tone of the critic and tore down the wall between us. Knocking down that barrier created openings for conversation, for questioning, for learning on both sides.

In summary:

- Do not fall into the trap of arguing about matters of taste.
- Do not, as a reflex, defend your work against negative criticism.
- Explain to your critic what you were trying to do.
- Transform arguments into conversations.

Not long ago, I found myself in a large bookstore where I stumbled on what turned out to be a writers' group. About a dozen adult writers sat in a tight circle, listening to a young man read a passage from his recent work. After the reading, the other members picked it apart. They accused the writer of misusing words, of writing too much description or not enough. I resisted the powerful urge to jump into the circle and indict them for their petty negativity. What stopped me was the reaction of the writer: he gazed into the eyes of each critic, nodded in understanding, jotted down the remark, and offered thanks. He was grateful for any response that would help him sharpen his tools, even when that response bordered on the insensitive.

Take a lesson from this earnest young writer. Even when an attack is personal, in your mind deflect it back onto the work: "What was it in the story that would provoke such anger?" If you can learn to use criticism in positive ways, you will continue to grow as a writer.

## WORKSHOP

1. Remember a time when someone delivered harsh criticism of your writing. Write down the criticism. Force yourself to write down something you learned from it that you can apply to future work.

2. Using the same example of criticism, write a memo to your critic explaining what you were trying to accomplish by writing the story the way you did.

3. Be your own harshest critic. Review a batch of your stories and write down ways that each could have been better, not what was wrong with them.

4. People tend to be harsher and more insensitive when they deliver criticism from a distance via e-mail. The next time you receive criticism this way, resist the urge to fire back a response. Take some time to recover. Then practice the advice offered above: explain to your critic what you were trying to accomplish.

5. Writers often know what is wrong with their work when they hand it in. Sometimes we try to hide these weaknesses from others. What would happen if we began to express them as part of the writing and revising process? Perhaps this would change the nature of the conversation and get writers and their helpers working together. When you hand in a piece of writing, write a memo to yourself. List weak elements you can strengthen with the help of your editor.

—‹o›—

# Own the tools of your craft.

*Build a writing workbench to store your tools.*

I've designed this final chapter as a guide for you to build a work-bench to store your writing tools. So far, I have organized these tools into four parts. We began with nuts and bolts, things like the power of subject and verb, emphatic word order, and the difference between stronger and weaker elements in prose.

From there we moved to special effects, ways of using the language to create specific and intended cues for the reader. You learned how to overpower clichés with creativity, how to set the pace for the reader, how to use overstatement and understatement, how to emphasize showing over telling.

The next part offered sets of blueprints, plans for organizing written work to help both the writer and the reader. You learned the differences between reports and stories; how to plant clues for readers; how to generate suspense; how to reward readers for moving down the page.

This last part coalesced earlier strategies into reliable habits, routines that give you the courage and stamina to apply these tools. You learned how to transform procrastination into rehearsal; how to read with a purpose; how to help others and let them help you; how to learn from criticism.

One final step requires you to store all of your tools on the shelves of a metaphorical writer's workbench. I began learning how to do this back in 1983 when Donald Murray, the teacher to whom this book is dedicated, stood in front of a tiny seminar room in St. Petersburg, Florida, and wrote on a chalkboard a blueprint that forever changed the way I taught and wrote. It was a modest description of how writers worked, five words that revealed the steps authors followed to build any piece of writing. As I remember them now, his words were:

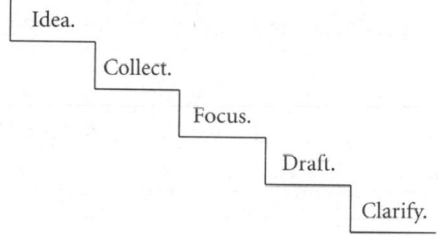

In other words, the writer conceives an idea, collects things to support it, discovers what the work is really about, attempts a first draft, and revises in the quest for greater clarity.

How did this simple blueprint change my writing life?

Until then, I thought great writing was the work of magicians. Like most readers, I encountered work perfected and published. I'd hold a book in my hand, flip through its pages, feel its weight, admire its design, and stand awestruck at its seeming perfection. This was magic, the work of wizards — people different from you and me.

Finished writing may seem magical, but I could now see the method behind the magic. I suddenly saw writing as a series of rational steps, a set of tools, and with the help of Murray's blueprint, I could construct a writer's workbench to store them. Writing teachers at the Poynter Institute have been trying to stock that workbench for more than twenty-five years now, cleaning it, expanding it, reorganizing it, adapting it to various writing and editing tasks. Here's my annotated version:

• *Sniff around.* Before you find a story idea, you get a whiff of something. Journalists call this a "nose for news," but all good writers express a form of curiosity, a sense that something is going on out there, something that teases your attention, something in the air.

• *Explore ideas.* The writers I admire most are the ones who see their world as a storehouse of story ideas. They are explorers, traveling through their communities with their senses alert, connecting seemingly unrelated details into story patterns. Most writers I know, even the ones who work from assignments, like to transform the topics of those assignments into their own focused ideas.

• *Collect evidence.* I love the wisdom that the best writers write not just with their hands, heads, and hearts, but with their feet. They don't sit at home thinking or surfing the Web. They leave their houses, offices, and classrooms. The great Francis X. Clines of the *New York Times* once told me that he could always find a story if he could just get out of the office. Writers, including writers of fiction, collect words, images, details, facts, quotes, dialogue, documents, scenes, expert testimony, eyewitness accounts, statistics, the brand of the beer, the color and make of the sports car, and, of course, the name of the dog.

• *Find a focus.* What is your essay about? No, what is it *really* about? Go deeper. Get to the heart of the matter. Break the shell and extract the nut. Getting there requires careful research, sifting through evidence, experimentation, and critical thinking. The focus of a story can be expressed in a title, a first sentence, a summary paragraph, a theme statement, a thesis, a question the story will answer for the reader, one perfect word.

• *Select the best stuff.* One great difference stands between new writers and experienced ones. New writers often dump their research into a story or essay. "By God, I gathered all that stuff," they think, "so it's going in." Veterans use a fraction, sometimes half, sometimes one-tenth of what they've gathered. But how do you decide what to include and, more difficult, what to leave out?

A sharp focus is like a laser. It helps the writer cut tempting material that does not contribute to the central meaning of the work.

• *Recognize an order.* Are you writing a sonnet or an epic? As Strunk and White ask, are you erecting a pup tent or a cathedral? What is the scope of your work? What shape is emerging? Working from a plan, the writer and reader benefit from a vision of the global structure of the story. This does not require a formal outline. But it helps to trace a beginning, middle, and ending.

• *Write a draft.* Some writers write fast and free, accepting the inevitable imperfection of early drafts, moving toward multiple revisions. Other writers, my friend David Finkel comes to mind, work with meticulous precision, sentence by sentence, paragraph by paragraph, combining the drafting and revising steps. One way is not better than another. But here's the key: I once believed that writing began with drafting, the moment my rear hit the chair and my hands hit the keyboard. I now recognize that step as deep in the process, a step that becomes more fluid when I have taken other steps first.

• *Revise and clarify.* Don Murray once gave me a precious gift, a book of photographed manuscript pages titled *Authors at Work.* In it you see the poet Percy Bysshe Shelley crossing out by hand the title "To *the* Skylark," revising it to "To *a* Skylark." You watch as the novelist Honoré de Balzac writes dozens upon dozens of revisions in the margins of a corrected proof. You can observe Henry James cross out twenty lines of a twenty-five-line manuscript page. For these artists, writing is rewriting. And while word processors now make such revisions harder to track, they also eliminate the donkey labor of recopying and help us improve our work with the speed of light.

Sniff. Explore. Collect. Focus. Select. Order. Draft. Revise.

Don't think of these as tools. Think of them as tool shelves or toolboxes. A well-organized garage has the gardening tools in one corner, the paint cans and brushes in another, the car repair equipment in another, the laundry helpers in another. In the same way, each of my process words describes a mode of writing and thinking that contains its own tool set.

So in my *focus box,* I keep a set of questions the reader may ask about the story. In my *order box,* I have story shapes such as the chronological narrative and the gold coins. In my *revision box,* I keep my tools for cutting useless words.

A blueprint of the writing process will have many uses over time. Not only will it give you confidence by demystifying the act of writing, not only will it provide you with big boxes in which to store your tool collection, but it will also help you diagnose problems in individual stories. It will help you account for your strengths and weaknesses over time. And it will build your critical vocabulary for talking about your craft, a language about language that will lead you to the next level.

## WORKSHOP

1. With some friends, take a big piece of chart paper and with colored markers draw a diagram of your writing process. Use words, arrows, images, anything that helps open a window to your mind and method.

2. Find a piece of your writing that did not work. Using the writing tasks described above, identify the part of the process that broke down. Did you fail to collect enough information? Did you have a problem selecting the best material?

3. Using the tasks, create a scoring grid. Review a portfolio of your writing and grade yourself in each of the categories. Do you generate enough story ideas? Is your work well ordered?

4. Interview another writer about her writing process. Turn it into a conversation in which you describe your own methods.

5. On a blank piece of paper, list your favorite writing tools to add to this collection. Good luck and keep writing.

# AFTERWORD

─◀◉▶─

So there you have them: a shiny new set of writing tools and a workbench on which to store them. Use them well, to learn, to find your authentic voice, and to see the world — with startling intensity — as a storehouse of story ideas. Use them to become a better student, a better teacher, a better worker, a better parent, a better citizen, a better person. Own these writing tools. They now belong to you. Keep them sharp. Share them with others. Add your own. Take pride in your craft. Join a nation of writers. And never forget to get the name of the dog.

# Acknowledgments

—◄o►—

Writers who care about the craft owe a debt to Donald M. Murray, perhaps the most influential writing teacher in the nation's history. Don's fingerprints appear on many of these tools. I thank him for teaching me how to think of writing as a process, how to listen to writers, and how to gather tools for my workbench.

Thanks to Thomas French of the *St. Petersburg Times,* who has taught me so much about narrative, including how to build story engines, how to report for scenes, and how to place them in a meaningful sequence.

Don Fry has been my writing teacher for more than thirty-five years. He started as my graduate school mentor, became my friend and then my colleague. To sharpen my writing tools, I have borrowed Don's definition of voice along with his ideas on how to reward readers with "gold coins."

Christopher "Chip" Scanlan has taught me the value of freewriting, critical thinking, and planning, helping me tame that watcher at the gate, the critical voice that sounds in my brain, especially when I'm writing about writing.

My thanks to Carolyn Matalene, who taught at the University of South Carolina. Carolyn reintroduced me to the ladder of abstraction and warned me of the dangers of the middle rungs. She also encouraged me to study rhetorical grammar and helped me clarify the notion that the number of elements in a piece of writing has meaning.

I have worked with these inspirational teachers at the Poynter Institute, which has been my professional home since 1979. Poynter is the nonprofit school for journalists that owns the stock of the *St. Petersburg Times,* one of America's best newspapers. My career in Florida began when the legendary editor, Gene Patterson, transformed me from a young assistant professor of English into a writing coach. Karen Brown Dunlap and Keith Woods now preside over Poynter with a care and devotion that continue to inspire my best work.

My friends and helpers in St. Pete are too numerous to mention here. But I could not have produced the tools without the encouragement of Bill Mitchell and Julie Moos, who direct Poynter's world-famous Web site (www.poynter.org), and intern Elizabeth Carr, who remains number one in my book. Thanks to Kenny Irby for my author photo.

My gratitude extends to the many online writers and editors who have linked to the original versions of the tools, and to the thousands of readers who have offered support, encouragement, and deserved correction.

Many tools came from formative conversations with authors, poets, and journalists across the country. These have included Jacqui Banaszynski, Bill Blundell, David Finkel, Jon and Lynn Franklin, Jack Hart, Anne Hull, Kevin Kerrane, Mark Kramer, Kate Long, Peter Meinke, Howell Raines, Diana Sugg, David Von Drehle, Elie Wiesel, and Jan Winburn, to name a few.

Just as one generation of athletes borrows moves from an earlier one, so have I paid close attention to the authors who have written about writing. If you've read this book, you'll recognize my debt to Strunk and White, William Zinsser, Dorothea Brande, George Orwell, Rudolf Flesch, Anne Lamott, Max Perkins, Louise Rosenblatt, Frank Smith, Tom Wolfe, and many more.

From elementary school through graduate school, I've been educated by teachers and mentors who have nurtured me for years and years. These include Richard McCann, Bernard Horst, Richard Geraghty, Rene Fortin, Rodney Delasanta, Brian Barbour, John Hennedy, Paul Van K. Thomson, John Cunningham, Marty Stevens, and Guinavera Nance. Special thanks go to Mary Osborne and the late Janie Guilbault.

I owe at least one big apple and a crate of citrus to two marvelous New Yorkers. My agent, Jane Dystel, recognized the potential in this collection of writing tools and led me through the liturgies of publication with consummate professionalism, fun, and care. She also introduced me to Tracy Behar, who worked so hard to bring this book to Little, Brown. Under her wise and gentle direction, I was able to reimagine and reshape *Writing Tools* for the broadest possible audience. I can't imagine working with a more supportive editor.

My thanks go to all the dedicated and creative workers at Little, Brown under the leadership of publisher Michael Pietsch (pronounced "peach"): Sophie Cottrell, associate publisher; Heather Rizzo, publicity director; Bonnie Hannah, publicist; Mario Pulice, art director; Marilyn Doof, production manager; Meryl Sussman Levavi, freelance designer; Marie Salter, copyeditor; and Caitlin Earley. In its care of me, my publisher has been high minded and innovative, with a long-term vision for the life of a writing book.

Finally, I do believe that writing is a social activity, so thanks go to those closest to me: Pegie and Stuart Adam; Tom French and his sons; Kelly McBride and her family; the Morse family; Joe and Diane Tonelli; Sharon and Jared Mellon; my mother-in-law, Jeannette Major; my brothers, Vincent and Ted; my mother (and first editor), Shirley Clark; my daughters, Alison, Emily, and Lauren; my wife, Karen Clark; and, of course, with greatest affection, my Jack Russell terrier — whose name is Rex.

# Writing Tools Quick List

◄○►

Use this quick list of *writing tools* as a handy reference. Copy it and keep it in your wallet or journal, or near your desk or keyboard. Share it and add to it.

## Part One: Nuts and Bolts

1. Begin sentences with subjects and verbs.
   *Make meaning early, then let weaker elements branch to the right.*
2. Order words for emphasis.
   *Place strong words at the beginning and at the end.*
3. Activate your verbs.
   *Strong verbs create action, save words, and reveal the players.*
4. Be passive-aggressive.
   *Use passive verbs to showcase the "victim" of action.*
5. Watch those adverbs.
   *Use them to change the meaning of the verb.*

6. Take it easy on the *-ings.*
    *Prefer the simple present or past.*
7. Fear not the long sentence.
    *Take the reader on a journey of language and meaning.*
8. Establish a pattern, then give it a twist.
    *Build parallel constructions, but cut across the grain.*
9. Let punctuation control pace and space.
    *Learn the rules, but realize you have more options than you think.*
10. Cut big, then small.
    *Prune the big limbs, then shake out the dead leaves.*

### Part Two: Special Effects

11. Prefer the simple over the technical.
    *Use shorter words, sentences, and paragraphs at points of complexity.*
12. Give key words their space.
    *Do not repeat a distinctive word unless you intend a specific effect.*
13. Play with words, even in serious stories.
    *Choose words the average writer avoids but the average reader understands.*
14. Get the name of the dog.
    *Dig for the concrete and specific, details that appeal to the senses.*
15. Pay attention to names.
    *Interesting names attract the writer — and the reader.*
16. Seek original images.
    *Reject clichés and first-level creativity.*
17. Riff on the creative language of others.
    *Make word lists, free-associate, be surprised by language.*
18. Set the pace with sentence length.
    *Vary sentences to influence the reader's speed.*

19. Vary the lengths of paragraphs.
    *Go short or long — or make a turn — to match your intent.*
20. Choose the number of elements with a purpose in mind.
    *One, two, three, or four: each sends a secret message to the reader.*
21. Know when to back off and when to show off.
    *When the topic is most serious, understate; when least serious, exaggerate.*
22. Climb up and down the ladder of abstraction.
    *Learn when to show, when to tell, and when to do both.*
23. Tune your voice.
    *Read stories aloud.*

## Part Three: Blueprints

24. Work from a plan.
    *Index the big parts of your work.*
25. Learn the difference between reports and stories.
    *Use one to render information, the other to render experience.*
26. Use dialogue as a form of action.
    *Dialogue advances narrative; quotes delay it.*
27. Reveal traits of character.
    *Show character-istics through scenes, details, and dialogue.*
28. Put odd and interesting things next to each other.
    *Help the reader learn from contrast.*
29. Foreshadow dramatic events and powerful conclusions.
    *Plant important clues early.*
30. To generate suspense, use internal cliffhangers.
    *To propel readers, make them wait.*
31. Build your work around a key question.
    *Stories need an engine, a question that the action answers for the reader.*

32. Place gold coins along the path.
    *Reward the reader with high points, especially in the middle.*
33. Repeat, repeat, and repeat.
    *Purposeful repetition links the parts.*
34. Write from different cinematic angles.
    *Turn your notebook into a camera.*
35. Report and write for scenes.
    *Then align them in a meaningful sequence.*
36. Mix narrative modes.
    *Combine story forms using the broken line.*
37. In short works, don't waste a syllable.
    *Shape short writing with wit and polish.*
38. Prefer archetypes to stereotypes.
    *Use subtle symbols, not crashing cymbals.*
39. Write toward an ending.
    *Help readers close the circle of meaning.*

### Part Four: Useful Habits

40. Draft a mission statement for your work.
    *To sharpen your learning, write about your writing.*
41. Turn procrastination into rehearsal.
    *Plan and write it first in your head.*
42. Do your homework well in advance.
    *Prepare yourself for the expected — and unexpected.*
43. Read for both form and content.
    *Examine the machinery beneath the text.*
44. Save string.
    *For big projects, save scraps others would toss.*
45. Break long projects into parts.
    *Then assemble the pieces into something whole.*
46. Take an interest in all crafts that support your work.
    *To do your best, help others do their best.*
47. Recruit your own support group.
    *Create a corps of helpers for feedback.*

48. Limit self-criticism in early drafts.
    *Turn it loose during revision.*
49. Learn from your critics.
    *Tolerate even unreasonable criticism.*
50. Own the tools of your craft.
    *Build a writing workbench to store your tools.*

For more information on *Writing Tools,* see the Web sites for the Poynter Institute (www.poynter.org/writingtools) and Little, Brown and Company (www.HachetteBookGroupUSA.com). To purchase a copy of *Writing Tools,* visit your local or online bookstore.

# INDEX

—◄o►—

# About the Author

By some accounts, Roy Peter Clark is America's writing coach, devoted to creating a nation of writers. A PhD in medieval literature, he is widely considered the most influential writing teacher in the rough-and-tumble world of newspaper journalism. With a deep background in traditional media, Clark has illuminated the discussion of writing on the Internet. He has gained fame by teaching writing to children, and has nurtured Pulitzer Prize–winning authors such as Thomas French and Diana Sugg. He is a teacher who writes, and a writer who teaches.

For more than three decades, Clark has taught writing at the Poynter Institute, a school for journalists in St. Petersburg, Florida, considered among the most prominent such teaching institutions in the world. He graduated from Providence College with a degree in English and earned a PhD from Stony Brook University.

In 1977 he was hired by the *St. Petersburg Times* as one of America's first writing coaches and worked with the American Society of Newspaper Editors to improve newspaper writing nationwide. Because of his work with ASNE, Clark was elected as a distinguished service member, a rare honor for a journalist who has never edited a newspaper. He was inducted into the Features Hall of Fame, an honor he shares with Ann Landers.

Clark has authored or edited sixteen books about writing and journalism, including his most recent, *The Glamour of Grammar*. Humorist Dave Barry has said of him: "Roy Peter Clark knows more about writing than anybody I know who is not currently dead." He lives with his family in St. Petersburg, Florida.

# . . . And His Next Book

Look for *The Glamour of Grammar*, published by Little, Brown and Company. Following is the book's table of contents and an excerpt.

# Contents

• • •

*Introduction: Embrace grammar as
powerful and purposeful.*

**Part One.  WORDS**

8. Learn seven ways to invent words.

9. Become your own lexicographer.

10. Take advantage of the short-word economy of English.

11. Learn when and how to enrich your prose with foreign words.

### Part Two. POINTS

12. Use the period to determine emphasis and space.

13. Advocate use of the serial comma.

14. Use the semicolon as a "swinging gate."

15. Embrace the three amigos: colon, dash, and parentheses.

16. Let your ear help govern the possessive apostrophe.

17. Take advantage of the versatility of quotation marks.

18. Use the question mark to generate reader curiosity and narrative energy.

19. Reclaim the exclamation point.

20. Master the elliptical art of leaving things out.

21. Reach into the "upper case" to unleash the power of names.

22. Vary your use of punctuation to create special effects.

### Part Three. STANDARDS

23. Learn to *lie* or *lay*, as well as the principles behind the distinction.

## Part Five. PURPOSE

...

# Embrace grammar as powerful and purposeful.

My first rock 'n' roll record, a heavy 78 rpm vinyl disk, was "Hound Dog" by Elvis Presley. Most of the adults I knew thought that rock was "the devil's music," the pathway to moral degeneracy and juvenile delinquency. Even worse, they thought it would screw up our grammar. When they heard the King growl "You ain't nothin' but a hound dog," the grown-ups would holler: "There ain't no such word as 'ain't.'" Not to mention that double negative: "Well, if you ain't *nothin'*, then you must be *somethin'.*"

Back then, our parents and teachers subscribed to the school of grammar we all learned in, well, grammar school. They framed grammar as a strict set of rules we must master in order to use language "correctly." I did not know it then, but this school of grammar had a name. It was called *prescriptive* because it prescribed proper ways to use the English language.

I was an eighth grader at St. Aidan School in 1961, the year *Webster's Third* included the word *ain't*—without disapproval—for the first time. The conservators of language were outraged, denouncing the dictionary as a glorification of ignorance, and its editors as "permissive." But the *Webster's* team was doing nothing more or less than taking note of the way people actually used the language. These lexicographers were members of the *descriptive* school because they described the language used in spoken and written English.

More than a half century later, the grammar wars rage on, with the prescribers and describers professing antagonistic visions of what constitutes grammar, how it is learned, and how it should be taught. It is in this contentious context that I offer for your consideration *The Glamour of Grammar*.

If you are holding this book in your hands, it means that the English language lives inside you. That is a wonderful gift, one that many of you learned from the cradle, one that will grow with you until you whisper "Rosebud" or whatever your final word happens to be. But you have an even greater power at your fingertips. It comes not when your language lives inside you, but when you begin to live inside your language.

To help you live that life, this book invites you to embrace grammar in a special way, not as a set of rules but as a box of tools, strategies that will assist you in making meaning as a reader, writer, or speaker. Living inside the language requires a grammar of purpose, a grammar of effect, a grammar of intent. This type of grammar puts language into action. It doesn't shout at you, "No, no, no," but gives you a little push and says, "Go, go, go." This type of grammar enables us to practice the three behaviors that mark us as literate human beings: it helps us write with power, read with a critical eye, and talk about how meaning is made.

These reflections lead me to the purpose of this book's fabulous title, *The Glamour of Grammar*. At first glance, the phrase must seem oxymoronic, as paradoxical as a sequined pocket protector. Was there ever in the popular imagination a word less glamorous than *grammar*? But what if I were to tell you that at one time in the history of our language, *grammar* and *glamour* were the same word? Need proof? Let's consult the *Oxford English Dictionary*.

The bridge between the words *glamour* and *grammar* is magic. According to the *OED*, *glamour* evolved from *grammar* through an ancient association between learning and enchantment. There was a time when grammar described not just language knowledge but all forms of learning, which in a less scientific age included things like magic, alchemy, astrology, even witchcraft.

Evan Morris, editor and publisher of "The Word Detective," leads us through the maze:

> "Glamour" and "Grammar" are essentially the same word. In classical Greek and Latin, "grammar" (from the Greek "grammatikos," meaning "of letters") covered the whole of arts and letters, i.e., high knowledge in general. In the Middle Ages, "grammar" was generally used to mean "learning," which at the time included, at least in the popular imagination, a knowledge of magic. The narrowing of "grammar" to mean "the rules of language" was a much later development, first focusing on Latin, and only in the 17th century extended to the study of English and other languages.
>
> Meanwhile, "grammar" had percolated into Scottish English (as "gramarye"), where an "l" was substituted for an "r" and the word eventually became "glamour," used to mean specifically knowledge of magic and spells.

Even though the association between *grammar* and *glamour* is surprising, it's not hard to find a trail of connections leading to modern usage. In popular gothic stories detailing the misadventures of witches and vampires, the word *glamor* (without a *u*)—as both a noun and a verb—describes a magic spell that puts someone in a trance or makes a person forget. When we see a glamorous movie star walking down a red carpet, don't we sometimes hear the words *magical, alluring,* and *enchanting?*

The word *grammar* has taken a bit of a nosedive since the days when some tipsy scholar north of Hadrian's Wall mixed up his *r*'s with his *l*'s. Today *grammar* connotes everything unglamorous: absentminded professors; fussy schoolteachers; British grammazons with binding names like Lynne Truss; nagging perfectionists; pedantic correctionists; high-school students asleep at their desks, stalactites of drool hanging from their lips. Long lost from grammar are associations with power, magic, enchantment, and mystical energy.

I've written *The Glamour of Grammar* so that you can feel that energy and put it to use. You will be guided by the broadest definition of *grammar* possible, used here to include pronunciation, spelling, punctuation, syntax, usage, lexicography, etymology, language history, diction, semantics, rhetoric, literature, and poetics. Words and definitions that now seem strange to you will become familiar and practical.

I've organized the grammar tools into these simple parts, extending from the subatomic level of language to the metaphysical:

**Part One. Words:** These tools deal with the smallest units of meaning: sounds, letters, symbols, words that help turn thought into language. You'll discover that no distinction is too small, that parts of speech can cross-dress, and that language is a source of limitless creativity.

**Part Two. Points:** To work together, words need help. They need connecting words, and they need punctuation. All methods of punctuation point the way for the reader, gathering, linking, separating, and emphasizing what truly matters. These marks are more than squiggles on the page. They are the ligaments of meaning and purpose.

**Part Three. Standards:** To make meaning with clarity and consistency, users of language lean on conventions, sets of informal agreements about what constitutes proper and improper usage. Violations of these are often perceived as errors. But to describe these standards as "rules" is to underestimate their value. As "tools" they offer strategic options for the speaker, reader, and writer.

**Part Four. Meaning:** Most human beings are born with the capacity to create an infinite number of sentences, each with the potential to capture meaning in a powerful way. While the number of sentences may be limitless, their forms are limited enough so that we can master them and influence how meaning is made and how it is experienced in the minds of an audience.

**Part Five. Purpose:** The tools of language, it turns out, are morally neutral, which is to say that good people can use them for good effects, and bad people can use them to lie, exploit, even to enslave. Living inside the language enables you to use grammar with a mission, to embrace ways of reading, writing, and speaking that inspire virtues such as justice, empathy, and courage.

With its practical and purposeful approach, *The Glamour of Grammar* tries to make grammar useful and memorable. Every little lesson in this book points to an immediate application. A feature called "Keepsakes" ends each chapter, reviewing the most important points in ways that can be saved, savored, and remembered, and offering a few fun exercises. Why learn grammar if you're not going to use it with intent? Why spell except to symbolize spoken words and avoid distracting the reader? Why punctuate except to point the reader toward pace, emphasis, and meaning? Why learn to identify subjects and verbs unless you can join them to achieve a specific effect?

I hope that this rhetorical grammar will help you grow in confidence and understanding so that you can master the rules, turn them into tools, and use those tools to break the rules with a purpose. On the inside, language will feel like muscle, not magic. I hope you will come to identify with my enthusiasm (a word that once meant "to have God in you"), just as I identify with lovers of the language such as Bryan A. Garner, author and editor of *A Dictionary of Modern American Usage,* who in my opinion is an apostle of a grammar of intent:

> The reality I care about most is that some people will want to use the language well. They want to write effectively; they want to speak effectively. They want their language to be graceful at

times and powerful at times. They want to understand how to use words well, how to manipulate sentences, and how to move about *in the language* without seeming to flail. They want *good grammar,* but they want more: they want *rhetoric* in the traditional sense. That is, they want to use the language deftly so that it's *fit for their purposes.* [my emphasis]

That paragraph makes the perfect distinction between rules and tools. It helps me understand that my interests in the technical aspects of language extend beyond simple correctness. I want to use these tools for effect, to help the reader learn, laugh, cringe, and turn the page.

For the lover of language, lessons come from everywhere, as British novelist and scholar David Lodge describes: "That is why a novelist...must have a very keen ear for other people's words...and why he cannot afford to cut himself off from low, vulgar, debased language; why nothing linguistic is alien to him, from theological treatises to backs of cornflakes packets, from the language of the barrack room to the language of, say, academic conferences." I got that message, even at age eight, when my teacher was Elvis Presley. By age thirteen, I was buried in hagiography and pornography; treatises on politics and stories about vampires; holy cards and baseball cards; scholarly books and comic books; the highest and the lowest our culture had to offer. I was living inside the English language.

# Use the semicolon as a "swinging gate."

My wife, Karen, worked with cancer patients for many years and taught me that an essential part of recovery is a good sense of humor. So when our pastor, Father Robert Gibbons, announced to the congregation that he'd need surgery for colon cancer, I rushed up to him after Mass with this happy thought: "Father, by the time they're finished with you, you may be the only man in America who knows how to use a semicolon."

The joke had the desired effect on the brainy cleric: it made him laugh.

Come to think of it, the semicolon does look a little like a colon with a polyp. In truth, it is probably used more often these days in winking emoticons ;-) than as an alternative to the period or the comma. Maybe because a period sits atop a comma in the semicolon, it sends off a "neither here nor there" aura, threatening me with its indifference.

Whenever I'm having unsettled thoughts about punctuation, I turn to the work of Tom Wolfe. It was in the 1960s, after all, when Wolfe and his buddies began to bust the boundaries of conventional nonfiction. Among those innovations was a tendency to use punctuation like hot spice in a Cajun stew. A little this!...A little that*!*!...Bada boom!!!

So, on a whim, I pulled out a copy of Wolfe's 1998 novel, *A Man in Full,* and thumbed through it until my eye caught this passage on page 262:

> Outside, Conrad threw the newspaper away in a receptacle on the corner. He now had two twenty-dollar bills, a five, a one, two quarters, a dime, and a nickel. He started walking again. Over there—a telephone. He deposited a quarter. Nothing; dead; it was out of order; he couldn't get the quarter back; he jiggled the lever; he pounded the machine with the heel of his hand. A panic rose up in him, and now his extremities seemed to shrink and grow cold. He walked all the way back to the first telephone he had found. His heart was beating much too fast. Gingerly he deposited his last quarter—and placed another collect call to Jill—and told her the whole sad story.

I admire this paragraph for many reasons, but especially for the ambitious varieties of punctuation, including ten periods, seven commas, five semicolons, and three dashes. I am especially intrigued by the unusual use of the semicolon in that central sentence:

> Nothing; dead; it was out of order; he couldn't get the quarter back; he jiggled the lever; he pounded the machine with the heel of his hand.

I admit that I would have been tempted to replace each semicolon with a period. In its current form, the sentence seems unparallel and out of joint. But then, isn't that the point of the sentence? In a panic, a man without a cell phone needs coins and a working pay phone to make an important human connection. By means of those semicolons, Wolfe describes a frantic series of actions that proceed in chronological order and together form a single sentence, a complete thought.

Abandoning Wolfe, I went from author to author looking for semicolons and was surprised to see the radically different preferences of writers, scholars, and critics. A collection of essays by twentieth-century philosopher Hannah Arendt revealed very few among hundreds of pages, while cultural critic Greil Marcus relies on them again and again, especially when he is trying to connect/divide two short important points: "Innocence is the colorless stain on the national tapestry," he writes in *The Shape of Things to Come.* "It violates the landscape; the only way to kill it is to cut it out."

Or "Alone, Madison plays a third video that has turned up. Like the first two, it opens in black and white; then in color it shows him kneeling on his bedroom floor."

Or "In his cell Madison has a vision of a house on stilts set in sand, burning; then the smoke and fire are sucked back into the house with a snap."

What strikes me about these uses of the semicolon is their arbitrariness, as if the semicolon were a mark of choice rather than of rule. Let me demonstrate the array of options inspired by the Marcus sentence "The Swede is the good son; Jerry is the bad son."

But why not "The Swede is the good son. Jerry is the bad son."

Or "The Swede is the good son, but Jerry is the bad son."

Or "The Swede is the good son, Jerry the bad son."

Or, with some subordination, "While the Swede is the good son, Jerry is the bad son."

If none of those possibilities is incorrect, then what impulse governs the writer? It sounds to me as if the writer is left with a musical decision. To the ear of Marcus, the semicolon without conjunction creates a balance achieved by simultaneous connection and separation.

What kind of object connects and separates at the same time? I suppose there are a number of correct answers, including the Cross Your Heart bra, but I'm thinking more of the swinging gate. That's how I see the semicolon in my own writing, as a gate that stands between two thoughts, a barrier that forces separation but invites you to pass through to the other side.

The French call the semicolon the *point-virgule,* which means something like the "point comma," and they have been fighting over it for a long time, as only the frisky and fractious French can. A French satirist named François Cavanna exclaims that the semicolon is "a parasite, a timid, fainthearted, insipid thing, denoting merely uncertainty, a lack of audacity, a fuzziness of thought." On the other side, reports Jon Henley of the *Guardian,* are those French triumphalists who see the semicolon as expressive of a nuance and delicate ambiguity of which Anglo writers are incapable.

New York standard-bearers went gaga when reporter Sam Roberts found a semicolon in this subway sign: "Please put it in a trash can; that's good news for everyone." Comments Roberts in the *New York Times:* "Semicolon sightings in the city are unusual, period, much less in exhortations drafted by committees of civil servants. In literature and journalism, not to mention in advertising, the semicolon has been largely jettisoned as a pretentious anachronism."

But one person's pretentious anachronism may be another's timely solution. So when would I use the semicolon in my own writing? My choices are governed more by sight than sound, especially on those occasions when the run of the sentence threatens to overflow the banks established by weaker forms of punctuation. Consider this autobiographical passage:

> Growing up a baseball fan in New York in the 1950s was to be engaged in an endless debate with neighbors on who was baseball's greatest center fielder: Duke Snider of the Dodgers, who was a sturdy defender and one of the most reliable sluggers in the league; or Willie Mays of the Giants, one of baseball's first great black superstars, a man who on any given day could astonish you with his bat or his glove; or my idol, Mickey Mantle, the Yankee heir to the crown of Joe DiMaggio, who, when he was healthy, could run faster and hit the ball farther than anyone who ever played the game.

used only commas in that rambling and energetic sentence, there would have been ten of them, too many to help the reader keep track of its parts. When I substituted semicolons, the parts became clear. You can see them with your eye: a topic clause, followed by one part Duke, one part Willie, one part the Mick.

There remains a place for the semicolon even at a time, according to English professor Jennifer DeVere Brody, when the misunderstood mark "suffers nightmares from its precarious position" between the period and the comma. Perhaps it will be saved by the likes of poet Maurya Simon, who has her own peculiar dreams about punctuation:

> The semicolon is
> Like a sperm forever frozen in its yearning towards an
>     ovum,
> like a tadpole swimming upstream to rouse the moon's
>     dropped coin...

An author who likens a semicolon to a sperm—now that's what I call a sex symbol—is living a life deep inside the English language.

## KEEPSAKES

• The semicolon, long the subject of neglect and ridicule, may be making a comeback.

• It offers the writer choices other than the comma, period, or dash.

• Think of the semicolon as a "swinging gate," a tool that can connect and separate at the same time.

• A long passage with lots of commas may confuse the reader. Consider the semicolon a mark that offers the reader a visual clue as to how a passage is organized.